What Research Says to the Science Teacher

Volume Six

The Process of Knowing

Mary Budd Rowe, editor

National Science Teachers Association

This book has been edited and produced by the staff of Special Publications, the National Science Teachers Association, 1742 Connecticut Avenue, N.W., Washington, D.C. 20009. Shirley Watt Ireton, Managing Editor; Cheryle L. Shaffer, Assistant Editor; Gregg Sekscienski, Editorial Assistant.

Library of Congress Catalog Card Number 90-061867

Stock Number PB–37/6
ISBN Number 0-87355-093-5

Printed in the United States of America
First edition

Volume 6
What Research Says to the Science Teacher
The Process of Knowing

Acknowledgments

As we bring you *What Research Says to the Science Teacher—The Process of Knowing*, we would like to thank the many people whose contributions and support have made this publication possible. We give special thanks to the preservice teachers and experienced teachers in Mary Budd Rowe's Learning and Instruction class, who spent a semester studying and critiquing this manuscript. We also appreciate the efforts of Diane Brady and Jim Strandquist of the Prince George's County, Maryland school system in providing us with some of the more difficult to find textbooks.

Finally we express our gratitude to the many publishers who aided us in this process by allowing us to duplicate figures in our publication.

Figure 1
From: BSCS *Biological Science: An Inquiry into Life*, 4th ed., 1980, Figure 3-17, (p. 90), Copyright 1980 by Biological Sciences Curriculum Study.

Figure 2a
From: *Biology: Living Systems*, 4th ed., (p. 75), by R. F. Oram, 1983, Columbus, OH: Charles E. Merrill. Copyright 1983 by Charles E. Merrill.

Figure 2b
From: *Biology*, (p. 102), by H. D. Goodman, T. C. Emmel, L. E. Graham, F. M. Slowiczek, and Y. Schechter, 1986, Orlando, FL: Harcourt, Brace, Jovanovich. Copyright 1986 by Harcourt, Brace, Jovanovich.

Figure 2c
From: *Modern Biology*, (p. 67), by A. Towle, 1989, Austin, TX: Holt, Rinehart & Winston. Copyright 1989 by Holt, Rinehart & Winston.

Figure 2d
From: *Heath Biology*, (p.71), by J. E. McLaren and L. Rotundo, 1985, Lexington, MA: D. C. Heath and Company. Copyright 1985 by D.C. Heath and Company.

Figure 2e
From: *Biological Science: A Molecular Approach*, Blue Verson, Fifth ed., (p. 128, figure 6-12), by Toby Klang (Ed.), 1985, Lexington, MA: D. C. Heath and Company. Copyright 1985 by D. C. Heath and Company.

Figure 3
This figure is from *The World of Cells*, (p. 329), by W. Becker, 1986, Palo Alto, CA: Benjamin/Cummings. This figure is in turn based upon a figure from *The Journal of Cell Biology*, 1975, vol. 67, p. 835, by copyright permission of the Rockefeller University Press. Permission also granted by G. Blobel and B. Dobberstein.

Introduction

This volume of *What Research Says to the Science Teacher* focuses on the implications of cognitive science research for improvement of education in the sciences. How can we best assist "the process of knowing"?

James Connor in Chapter One examines a question not usually cast in a cognitive context, namely, How can we more effectively link the intended (planned) curriculum and the learned curriculum (the one that goes out the school door in the heads of our students)? Where should the locus of curriculum development be? One faction argues it should start within the disciplines. Another camp—science, technology, society (STS) supporters—urges us to ground curriculum in more socially and psychologically compelling contexts. In any case, Connor invites our attention to the problem of reducing the gap between the planned and the learned curriculum. In one way or another, the remaining chapters in this monograph address some aspect of that problem.

Textbooks carry a piece of the curriculum message. Some of what texts teach may fit the planned curriculum, but Robert Blystone shows us some unintentional misrepresentations that creep into illustrations. Texts need more and better illustrations than they currently have. Blystone is very specific about the kinds of purposes illustrations should accomplish. His chapter provides guidance for evaluating illustrations, for designing better ways of presenting information in texts, and for using illustrations in teaching.

Teachers are the main arbiters between the intended curriculum and the learned curriculum. Edward Smith examines the way they go about the business of bringing the planned curriculum and the learned curriculum into closer relation. They have their own ways of thinking about the content and context of instruction. They enact their roles according to how they think about the situation—and there is more than one way to do that. He suggests some changes in preservice, inservice, and school administration practices that would help teachers transmit the intended curriculum more effectively.

When it comes to science the gap between the intended curriculum and the learned curriculum is greater for girls than it is for boys. Jane Butler Kahle has spent a good many years trying to understand why that is. In her chapter, Kahle claims that the problem is cultural, and she focuses on the creation of contexts which support intellectual adventuring by young females. She identifies things that people can do to improve this situation.

Heather Brasell's chapter on graphing brings again to a theme discussed by Blystone, namely, illustrations. In this case, however, she focuses on graphs and graphing as a means of communicating information and portraying relationships. She identifies specific kinds of trouble students have in interpreting and constructing graphs. She strongly advocates the use of graphs, particularly in real-time data contexts in the laboratory and recommends a number of procedures for strengthening graphing skill and comprehension.

Students often come to science classes with strong pre-instructional concepts about how things in nature work. They form these ideas first hand as a result of experience and apparently do so quite spontaneously. In class, however, they may encounter a different way of explaining what they took to be familiar phenomena. Discrepancies between the home-grown view and the science view cause difficulty in learning if they are not straightened out early in the course. The problem is that the home-grown ideas, as Mary Budd Rowe and Cynthia Holland point out, are resistant to change. Rowe and Holland argue for early identification of counterintuitive ideas or misconceptions. To bridge the gap between the intended and learned curriculum it will be necessary to design instruction to counter these views directly.

In the last chapter Gilbert Burney and William Popejoy focus on one possible source of the gap between the intended and the learned curriculum—the discrepancy between the demands of the planned program and the stage of the intellectual development of the students. To combat this problem, teachers need an easily administered and evaluated stage assessment instrument. Burney and Popejoy, working within a Piagetian framework, provide us with a test to measure formal thought capability. The instrument helps the user to distinguish formal from transitional and pre-formal development in students.

Mary Budd Rowe

About the Authors

Robert V. Blystone. A professor of biology at Trinity University in Texas, Blystone teaches courses in cell and molecular biology, microanatomy, and electron microscopy. His research interests are divided between cell biology and science education. He is currently producing computer-generated, three-dimensional images of viral-expressing mouse macrophage cells. Dr. Blystone is also developing histology and descriptive embryology labs that use computer produced images for introducing the histological material instead of the light microscope. He is a fellow of the American Association for the Advancement of Science, a member of NSTA and Sigma Xi, and a Piper Professor of Texas.

Heather M. Brasell. Currently, Brasell makes her home in rural Georgia and teaches chemistry and physics at Coffee High School. She received her B.S. from Massey University (New Zealand), B.A. from University of Queensland (Australia), M.S. from James Cook University (Australia), and Ph.D. from University of Florida in 1987. Before transferring to science education, Brasell was a forest ecologist with Commonwealth Scientific Industrial and Research Organization in North Queensland and Tasmania in Australia from 1974–82. Her science-education research interests have focused on graphing, misconceptions, and microcomputer-based labs.

Gilbert M. Burney. Reflecting his interest in math and computer science education, Burney currently teaches in the math department at Muscatine Community College. He received his Ed.D. in mathematics education from the University of Northern Colorado, his M.A. from the University of South Dakota, and his B.S. from South Dakota State University.

James V. Connor. Program Director for Science Education at New York University for the past several years, Connor did graduate work in physics at Catholic, Harvard, and Yale Universities and earned his doctorate in science education at Teacher's College, Columbia University. Since 1982, he has been the director of OUTREACH, an environmental and health awareness program for developing nations. Its goal is to provide free information on these issues to print and radio media with an emphasis on primary school children's magazines in Africa, Asia, and Latin America.

Beverly C. Dettling. A science-education graduate of Trinity University, Dettling did her undergraduate research on textbooks with Robert Blystone. Upon graduation, she entered the Peace Corps and has been working in Morocco for the past two years. Her current responsibility is to prepare orphans under the age of three for pre-K learning experiences.

Cynthia Holland. A teacher for 14 years in secondary schools in Indiana and Florida, Holland is currently working on her Ph.D. at the University of Florida. At the university level, she is involved in teacher training through workshops as well as through supervision of student teachers. She is also employed as a graduate research assistant for the Self Help ELementary Level Science videotape series funded by NSF.

Jane Butler Kahle. Past recipient of NSTA's STAR award and an international scholar in the area of gender issues, Kahle began her career teaching high-school biology in rural Indiana. Since earning her M.A. and Ph.D. in biology education from Purdue University, she has written or edited six books, fourteen chapters in books, and numerous papers. She has served as president of the National Association of Biology Teachers and as chairperson of the Board of Directors of the Biological Sciences Curriculum Study. She currently is chairperson of Section Q of the American Association for the Advancement of Science and president of National Association for Research in Science Teaching. Kahle's research focuses on factors affecting the entrance, retention, and achievement of females in science.

William D. Popejoy. With his B.S. and M.S. from Illinois State University and his Ed.D. from University of Northern Colorado, Popejoy currently teaches K–12 mathematics teacher education at the University of Northern Colorado. His research interests include cognitive psychology as applied to the learning and teaching of mathematics and science, and the development of a curriculum which matches the style and level of teaching material to the cognitive level of the learner.

Mary Budd Rowe. Past president of NSTA and former chairperson for Section Q of the American Association for the Advancement of Science, Rowe holds her Ph.D. from Stanford University. She is noted for her research on wait time—a technique involving pauses after a teacher's question and after the student's response which allows the student time to consider his/her response and also allows a teacher the same time to consider how to react. Rowe's research interests include the interaction of science and attitudes, particularly fate control and science achievement. She is currently a professor of science education at the University of Florida.

Edward L. Smith. Smith received a Ph.D. in Science Education from Cornell University in 1969. He has been on the faculty of Michigan State University since 1973, where he has pursued research on the teaching and learning of science. His research has examined both students' conceptions of natural phenomena and teachers' conceptions of science teaching and learning—and the influence these have on classroom instruction and learning.

1

Naive Conceptions and the School Science Curriculum

James V. Connor
New York University
New York, New York

Gladly did he teach and gladly learn.

—G. Chaucer

An old peasant woman once came to the large city school from her small village to enroll her youngest son. As the story goes, she begged the director to "learn my son—my village needs him." He replied that the school had a great reputation, that the faculty were well qualified, and that they would "teach" not "learn" her son. To this she answered that the school and faculty were well known for excellent teaching but that her son was not only to be taught, but learned—since his village needed him.

In this paper, the subtlety of the old peasant woman's intuition will be emphasized in terms of the curriculum. Yes, the school can decide on the curriculum (intended curriculum) and philosophize and dictate policy about it. But if the curriculum of the teachers in the classroom (implemented curriculum) and the curriculum of the students after leaving the classroom (achieved curriculum) are not considered, the children will only be taught, not learned.

This story in a simple way outlines the role of education in our society and, in fact, any society. The word education implies a "leading out" of something and into something else, or, as some would say, a conversation between generations. In general terms, effective education will focus on the needs of the individual and of the society, in our case a democratic one. While there are many ways of expressing these needs, a parallel will be set up in this paper between individual and societal needs with possible answers focusing on the needs of both from an educational perspective.

The broad goals and contexts for science education will be discussed in the first part of this paper. The limitations and possibilities of students with regard to meeting these goals will be discussed in the next section, and the limitations and possibilities of teachers will be discussed in the last section.

Intended Curriculum—Goals and Contexts

Goals. When we think about the general goals of education, which provide the framework for a curriculum, we normally think of goals that serve individuals and those directed to needs of the society, at large. From the standpoint of our society's needs, the primary goal of general education is to enable each person to become a responsible citizen in a democratic society. In this case, we usually mean one who is able to intelligently vote, who has the knowledge, skills, and outlook necessary to uphold the political and cultural values of the nation. Society's second major goal of general education is to enable each person to contribute to the economic and intellectual power of the country.

For our purposes, we will focus on scientific literacy, along with or incorporated into the general goal of basic literacy (the three R's). Just as there are many levels of general literacy, ranging from reading and understanding warning labels on medicines to Shakespeare and beyond; from writing checks to writing journal articles and novels, so too with scientific literacy. Scientific literacy has many levels within each of the usual divisions of knowledge, skills, and attitudes. Certainly everyone needs some scientific knowledge, some facts about the physical and biochemical world around us. Similarly one should know something about the relationships of science, technology, and society—yesterday, today, and tomorrow—with particular emphasis on the political, economic, and ethical dimensions.

The level of scientific literacy necessary for the average citizen is debatable, as is the level of general literacy (Hirsch, 1987; Shamos, 1988). But certainly we would want our families to be aware of the ingredients of the food we eat, the value of exercise, the warnings about smoking and cholesterol, the dangers of living near a nuclear plant or a toxic-waste site, and so on. We would also want our children to reach adulthood not only understanding the science behind such questions but willing to question, speak out, and vote intelligently on such issues. A major question is how to do some of this within our schools as efficiently as possible. To provide a partial answer, I will briefly consider what experts in the early 1980s thought should be the goals of science education in today's schools.

Project Synthesis was a major research effort funded by the National Science Foundation (NSF), directed by N. Harms, to interpret and synthesize three earlier major studies also funded by NSF concerning the status of science education (Helgeson, Blosser, and Howe, 1977; Stake and Easley, 1978; Weiss, 1978). An initial activity of Project Synthesis was to broadly identify the most fundamental goals of science education. The staff developed the term "goal cluster" to emphasize the impossibility of listing all the goals in a few statements. Harms and R. Yager assembled the information gathered through Project Synthesis into a monograph for the National Science Teachers Association (NSTA) (Harms and Yager, 1981). Four broad goal clusters and their implications described in the monograph are as follows (pp. 8–9):

1. *Personal Needs.* Science education should prepare individuals to use science to improve their own lives and to cope with an increasingly technological world.

2. *Societal Issues.* Science education should produce informed citizens prepared to deal responsibly with science-related societal issues.

3. *Career Education Awareness.* Science education should give all students an awareness of the nature and scope of a wide variety of science- and technology-related careers open to students of varying aptitudes and interests.

4. *Academic Preparation.* Science education should allow students who are likely to pursue science academically as well as professionally to acquire the academic knowledge appropriate for their needs.

At this time NSTA published a position paper asserting that a major goal of science education is to develop individuals who understand how science, technology, and society (STS) influence one another and who use this knowledge in their daily lives.

This theme was expanded into a list of 13 attributes that concurs with the four goal clusters of Project Synthesis, but the position statement placed more emphasis on the process skills (NSTA, 1985). The percentage of instructional time at various grade levels (K–12) which should be devoted to (a) process skills, (b) concept development, (c) application, and (d) science-based societal issues were presented as well. This general linking of science and technology with society was also advanced by a task force on curriculum assembled by the National Science Board Commission (NSF, 1983).

During the time these statements were made, there were several events of worldwide importance that substantiated the need for science, technology, and society (STS) links. The oil crisis of 1974 awakened the United States to its vulnerability in energy resources. Scientists and engineers began to look for better ways to tap alternative energy resources, such as the energy from the nucleus, the sun, ocean thermals, wind, and oil shale. Environmental catastrophes also raised the consciousness of the need for links between science, technology, and society. The radiation disasters at Three Mile Island and the U.S.-based company's chemical plant disaster in Bhopal, India were still vivid in people's memories when Europe's great Rhine was contaminated and the Chernobyl nuclear accident in Russia polluted air that moved over to Scandinavia and beyond. When the resulting radioactive milk from European cattle destined for Africa's developing nations was intercepted, the STS circle was complete, in global terms. And the circle continues each day as we read of another species endangered, another acre of rain forest cleared every few seconds, another city adding another huge slum, we know that STS links must be emphasized and considered most carefully. The key events relating human needs to the environment, replete with the problems affecting us all worldwide, provide the major direction for science education today.

Context: Science Education in the United States. Prior to World War I, the study of science was quite limited. Science was seen in the context of religious inspiration, as a source of vocabulary for memorization, and as a means to glorify the rural life over urbanization. Then, after World War I, the science of the city was accepted, and school texts emphasized central heating and electricity, refrigerators and gasoline engines. It was not until the end of World War II that President Roosevelt commissioned a report by V. Bush (1946), facing up to the national need for more science education. Bush's theme, "Science, The Endless Frontier," led to the beginning of NSF five years later and its subsequent teacher institutes and new school science programs.

When the Russians launched Sputnik in 1957, the United States took steps to upgrade the science curriculum by involving scientists, schools, and teachers in a massive curriculum development and teacher inservice effort. Then, the worry was that this country was losing its position in world leadership to Russia, and an immediate effort to train scientists was made in an attempt to recover that leadership. In this context the "race to the moon" was symbolic. And we won. We had trained our scientists and engineers well.

But today there is a different thrust coming from a more general criticism of our school system. In the last few years, many studies have underlined that the 1960s idea of excellence is not enough. We also need equity. No longer can we concentrate on an elite cadre of future scientists and engineers (mostly white and male) but rather on all students, future citizens, with a focus on those largely forgotten earlier—women and minorities.

Context of Science: Quantity and Quality. The cognitive issues in curriculum are tremendous. The amount of new scientific information reported every day would fill several books. Today almost two million scientists and engineers worldwide (Lederman, 1987) produce more information than ever before. And this information gets transmitted from one scientist to another by approximately 1,500 research journals as well as by numerous secondary sources. The information available is staggering. But how much of this information reaches our children, and who decides what they should be taught?

Science textbooks rarely portray the dynamic nature of science and engineering. Instead science in the classroom comes across as a static, completed list of results in the form of tables, theories, and laws. Even scientific journals misrepresent what science really is. The Nobel laureate in biology P. B. Medawar (1963) called them "a fraud," charging that the journals usually omit the really creative and imaginative part of science, the hypothesizing.

J. Conant (1951), the president of Harvard University, also decried the impression that science is static rather than dynamic, a noun rather than a verb, that the principles, laws, and theories are ends rather than means. In a 1958 study, G. Holton and D. H. Roller distinguished two aspects of science: "Private" science is science in the making, what the person does, while "public" science (as written about in journals and texts) is science of the institution, what has finally been accepted in the struggle for ideas.

To illustrate how public science is achieved in practice, T. Kuhn (1962) stressed the revolutionary aspect of science whereby the current structure or paradigm accepted by the scientific community eventually gives way to a new paradigm. A conceptual revolution begins when, in the process of normal science, enough anomalies or inconsistencies occur to cause a crisis in thought among scientists. Then, doing normal science that helps find and fit missing pieces in the puzzle of the existing paradigm is no longer satisfactory, and a new paradigm must be found. Many scientists, possibly overreacting to being described as mere puzzle solvers within a paradigm, do not subscribe to Kuhn's approach. Yet science educators easily see it as a valid and useful way for the student to approach science as it really is—personal, imaginative, dynamic. The question then is how to capture this dynamism within the science curriculum.

For philosophers of science these days, the major arguments concern what is "real." Are unobservable, theoretical entities like electrons real or only fictional models, useful constructs around which to organize experience? Are the theories themselves true in a literal sense, or are they only useful tools? While these questions of reality become most important in the realm of sub-atomic physics, far from the billiard-ball model of the atom seen in most textbooks, there is a major gap that must be faced if science education is to be honest. But when and how?

The Cognitive Context. In the late 1970s, studies began that involved the nature of students' knowledge prior to instruction and its impact on learning processes. These were small, in-depth investigations involving researchers from many countries. The studies were remarkable in that, for the first time, evidence was overwhelming that students brought a great deal of prior knowledge to school with them, which was learned not at school, but at home and in out-of-school experiences. Since these ideas often differed from conceptions employed by scientists, they have been called misconceptions, preconceptions, alternate conceptions, etc. They will be referred to here as naive science.

Valuable curricular lessons are currently being learned from the Children's Learning in Science Project at the University of Leeds, England (Driver, Guesne, and Tiberghien, 1985). A research program begun there in 1982 is based on the premise that knowledge is mind constructed. Several fields of inquiry are based on this: the learner as purposefully constructing meaning, the community of scientists as constructing scientific knowledge itself, and individuals as acting according to their beliefs and the meanings they construe in social situations (including classrooms and schools). Four books that effectively synthesize the findings about naive conceptions and

interpret them for curricular and instructional purposes are the following:
Driver et al. (1985); R. Osborne and P. Freyberg (1985); L. H. T. West and A. L.
Pines (1985); A. Champagne, R. Gunstone, and L. Klopfer (1985). The general
consensus agrees that naive science is seen as having the following general
characteristics:
- starts early, before school begins, then continues lifelong
- subtle, and often missed by teachers unaware of it
- separable, that is, school answers are not merged with personal answers
- stable, or robust, even after being disproved
- personal, in that each child writes different conclusions than others after
the same experience (each child sees the experience from his or her own point
of view and constructs a personal meaning)
- incoherent to the teacher, and often contradictory

Because of the persistent nature of naive science, research in cognitive
psychology suggests that science curricula might benefit from following a
spiral approach, in which scientific ideas begin as early as possible and are
repeated frequently. In this way, whatever remains of students' naive
conceptions would be confronted at various points in the students' training.
Another suggestion from this research is that the subject matter be
reorganized based on the students' conceptual framework rather than the way
the discipline has evolved. The logic of the historical framework often makes
no sense at all from the students' naive perspectives.

Achieved Curriculum—Students

Limitations. The limitations of the achieved curriculum—what the students
leave classroom and school with—have been made painfully obvious by the
National Assessment of Educational Progress and comparisons of the United
States with other nations. How do we compare with other nations more
successful in science education? One major difference is the use made of the
textbook in the United States. We fill our textbooks with fact after fact, to be
memorized and returned on tests, so that textbooks often carry the main
burden of teaching in our classrooms. Instruction becomes a review of that
content, and as a result, over half the schools in the United States use the
same two biology textbooks (Weiss, 1986). As a contrast, in Sweden or China,
texts are very thin; they focus on major concepts; they are illustrated with a
few examples; and the teacher develops the science vocabulary in context.

In order to improve education in the United States, research indicates that
the text-teacher relationship must change. Texts must not be used as
glossaries to be memorized, and rather than depending on texts, teachers will
need to plan and execute many activities aimed at conceptual development
and modification.

Possibilities. Rote memorization in our classrooms is no longer a possibility:
There is just too much factual information for any student, even the most
brilliant and dedicated, to master. We must begin to make changes in the
curricular content and approach as we begin to address problems in light of
naive conceptions. While no one national curriculum is envisioned here, all
curricula must meet certain basic criteria. They must be
- valid—emphasize genuine science and appropriate technology
- meaningful—focus on local issues that have global analogs, are currently
reported in newspaper and television, and are relevant to the students' world
- fruitful—are understandable by students, are accepted by teachers, are
related to other sciences, and are related to technological and social issues
- practical—are part of an institutional curriculum structure, are supported
by text and educational technology, and are supported by trade books,
newspapers, and magazines

Several elementary science programs, developed in the 60s and 70s, meet these basic criteria. The Conceptually Oriented Program in Elementary Science (COPES) used five powerful science principles in its K–6 sequence: Structure of Matter; Interaction and Change; Energy Conservation; Energy Degradation; and the Statistical View of the Universe. The Science Curriculum Investigation Study (SCIS) divides its program for grades 1–6 into two sequences: physical science and life science. The physical science sequence includes Material Objects, Interaction and Systems, Subsystems and Variables, Relative Position and Motion, Energy Sources, Models—Electric and Magnetic Interactions. The life science sequence includes Organisms, Life Cycles, Populations, Environments, Communities, and Ecosystems.

Could we not follow the precedent set by these curriculum projects and reject the current trend of curricula and textbooks that are laden with facts? As an alternative to memorization and regurgitation, a curriculum for grades K–12 that is organized around a few topics, the "Big Ideas" of science, might give a clearer focus to students and allow them to organize other topics, both scientific and non-scientific, around this core. The development of such a list would in itself be an excellent exercise.

The Big Ideas curriculum for STS concentrates on the interrelation of ideas, such as resources and energy, population and pollution, and has many advantages because it links together a significant number of the ideas needed to upgrade scientific literacy in our citizens in a compelling way. Society's great achievements and great disasters are both seen as emanating from technology based on science. We, society, should be in control of both. (See, e.g., the recommendations on STS content in Project Synthesis (Harms and Yager)).

Implemented Curriculum—Teachers, Texts, and Technology

Teacher Training. So far, we have been examining the goals for both a general education curriculum and for science education in particular. These goals help structure an idealized intended curriculum in the hopes that it comes close to the achieved curriculum taken away from the classroom by the students. Between the two curricula, however, is the central figure, the classroom teacher who controls the implemented curriculum. Fortunately, many of the concerns set forth in this paper so far are also those of science teachers. A recent nationwide study (Gabel, Samuel, Helgeson, McGuire, Novak, and Butzow, 1987) revealed that elementary teachers say they need to know about research on the following topics: hands-on activities, science content of the curriculum, cognitive development and learning styles, and problem solving and teaching strategy. Supporting the need for this research, F. Lawrenz (1986) documented the physical science misconceptions of elementary school teachers: They had naive conceptions similar to their own elementary school students. And the durability of naive conceptions into adulthood is certainly not unique to teachers.

Whether the training of teachers on the effective use of naive science findings is done by preservice or inservice courses or is self-taught, the procedure might well follow this schema: awareness, conceptualization, training in methods, and use in the classroom.

A good way for a teacher to become aware of naive science and some of its implications is to read the following books: *Children's Ideas in Science* (Driver et al., 1985) and *Learning in Science* (Osborne and Freyberg (Eds.), 1985). These books could well be followed by *Cognitive Structure and Conceptual Change* (West and Pines (Eds.), 1985) which covers the same ideas in a more formal, theoretical style and extends more into secondary school. In all three books, the authors use a large number of examples, often with extensive case studies, that make problems very real. Once the case studies are understood, teachers could interview their own students about their ideas of science, especially regarding phenomena already taught and learned. A "why" or "how" question will usually find a naive conception lurking below the surface.

Teachers must also have a conceptual model of the relationship of students' naive science with the science of the scientist. A useful way to think of the interaction of the student's naive concepts with the scientist's concepts is in terms of two vines (West and Pines, 1985, p. 4; Di Sessa, 1987). The scientist's vine comes from above (authority) and meets the student's vine coming from below (intuition). Depending on the nature of the two vines, they can interact in four or more ways

- conflict, where the student's reality is challenged
- congruence, where the new ideas enlarge the student's world-view
- symbolic knowledge, where there is little student knowledge existing
- unstructured, where all the student's knowledge is intuitive (p. 4)

A "generative learning" model for changing the student's view is given by Wittrock (1974) that emphasizes how students must themselves actively construct or generate meaning from sensory input. This model stresses three objectives: clarification of the pupils' existing views, modification of their views toward the current scientific view, and the consolidation of the scientific view within the student's background. A process for teaching generative learning follows a preliminary phase that ascertains student views with focus, challenge, and application stages that aim at bringing a student's views in line with current scientific views.

Teachers also need training in the methods and interview techniques in order to recognize and combat misconceptions. There are several useful procedures to familiarize teachers with the alternative concepts of students. Any of the methods mentioned below would be quite useful, depending on the maturity of the students.

• The interview about instances technique (Osborne and Freyberg, 1985, p. 6) attempts to explore the concept which a child associates with a particular label, for example plant. A series of line drawings is shown to each child. The child decides if a drawing is or is not a plant according to his/her meaning of the word. After an answer is received, the interviewer attempts to find reasons for the response.

• The interview about events technique (Osborne and Freyberg, 1985, p. 8) investigates students' ideas about everyday phenomena (e.g. reflection of light, condensation of water vapor). It often reveals the strange ideas many children have of the world.

• The free-sort task listed by Champagne et al. (1985, p. 163) requires students to categorize 17 physics concepts: acceleration, force, position, etc., with an example given of how seven non-physics terms could be classified. The example and the instruction serve to stress the absence of any one right answer.

• The tree-construction task asks students to construct a linear undirected graph (tree) of the same 17 concepts above. Students begin by writing and then connecting the two most related concepts with a line numbered "1." The next most related word is then written and connected by line "2." The resulting tree of 16 lines is supposed to show the semantic distance between concepts.

• The concept structuring analysis technique (ConSAT) also uses these same 17 concepts written on individual cards. The students are asked to identify the ones they recognize, define them, and then group them on paper in a way that shows relationship. The students later explain the reasons for their classifications in an interview.

• The word-association task asks students to generate as many free associations as possible for each of five concepts (force, mass, speed, inertia, and change of motion) within a minute. Then they are asked to use both the concept and associated word technique to expose the nature of their links.

• The demonstrate, observe, explain (DOE) task probes the student's cognitive structure by asking for a prediction of the outcome of a sequence of physical demonstrations and an explanation for the prediction. After the demonstration, students are asked to explain differences between their predictions and their observations.

Once the teacher is made aware of the children's naive science and how strongly it is retained, the question is what to use as the best remedy. As with most remedies within the art of teaching, different ones work with different children and different teachers in different ways. Osborne and Freyberg (1985, p. 103) analyze and compare several approaches to combat alternative views before developing their own generative learning model, which also has three teaching phases (focus, challenge, and application) preceded by an explicit teacher-preparation phase (pp. 108–110).

Another method which is very useful for an entire class of even 20 to 30 students working together is the investigative-colloquium method created by B. Lansdown, R. E. Blackwood, and P. F. Brandwein (1972). This method combines the hands-on exploratory approaches mentioned earlier with directed discussion among the students, usually seated in a large circle. The discussion technique is based on Vygotsky's studies in language, where the children talk about their observations, agree or disagree about the evidence and its implications, and decide what to write in their class record. It is a particularly useful technique since a student often tends to speak in public more naturally and often more confidently in the face of another student's contradictions rather than the teacher's. A skilled teacher can use the discussion to pinpoint the naive science opposed to the accepted scientific view and help the children move toward experiments that would help them decide on the view that supports the evidence.

Textbook. There is no secret among science educators about the preeminence of the textbook for teaching science at all levels. The Project Synthesis report (Harms and Yager, 1981), mentioned earlier in connection with the goals of science education, showed that over 90 percent of all science teachers use a science textbook over 90 percent of the time. The textbook is also the source for the science terms to be mastered for exams, the laws to be verified in lab, even the lecture material of the teacher. With experience, time, and interest, beginning teachers are able to rely less and less on the textbook to organize instruction, but with 90 percent of all teachers, even the experienced, using the textbook most of the time, it is important to consider the textbook in any plans for curricular change at the implementation level.

A recent analysis of 11 elementary science textbook series (90 percent of the national market) shows little recent change in terms of the four Project Synthesis goal clusters (Staver and Bay, 1987). Generally the analysis shows that most textbook prose focuses on academic science, with the personal goal cluster in second place, and the career and societal goal cluster far behind, receiving minor attention. These texts allocate only a small portion of space to activities/experiments, and even then the emphasis is almost totally academic with inquiry present in very limited forms at best.

Similar results were found in a study of 22 high-school level biology texts (Rosenthal, 1983). The emphasis on social issues decreased between 1963 and 1983 in sampled texts, and the bulk of this small emphasis focused on evolution, human health, and the social system of science.

Perhaps much more could be done if the emphasis in textbooks turns to the "Big Ideas in Science" or "Big Problems and Solutions" mentioned earlier.

How did they come about, what evidence is there for them, and what are their implications for us now and in the future? Then there would be a chance for scientific conceptions to take the place of naive conceptions as students unified their world view. For this to happen the texts would have to contain fewer facts but more experimental approaches to the facts; fewer laws but more challenges to make theories of the facts, presented or discovered. Under these guidelines, the text would be a resource for new ideas to discuss in class, new ways to think about problems, and new ways to think about science, technology, and society—a gift that will last long after graduation.

As mentioned earlier, however, a great deal of research and deliberation is needed about which big ideas are the most fruitful and most pervasive, and about which ideas are most needed to help guide modern technology and solve the world's problems. Furthermore, no research has been done on how people acquire a meaningful understanding of such pervasive principles. Trial testing needs to be done in these areas to find the appropriate structure and sequence for the subtopics within the larger K–12 framework.

A 1987 attempt to restructure general science topics at the sixth-grade level, based on moving from a small to a large theme, also has implications for organizing the K–12 curriculum. In this revision, the course begins with matter, moves to energy, then to energy for living things, life forms, and finally to the climates in which they live (Hamrick and Harty, 1987).

Development across grades and subjects also needs to be considered. If, for example, the atomic-molecular-particulate view of matter is to be stressed in junior-high school, how many exercises in elementary school are needed in heat, electricity, chemistry, etc., to help children see the scientist's conception? How can lessons in science be integrated with the humanities? What are the best motivators for science topics? What are the links to modern technology and possible solutions to some of the world's problems?

Hopefully, such approaches will sustain student interest as they reach the sixth grade or so, when interest levels often wane. They may need to be made aware of how those ideas have developed and changed and how the ideas relate to varying social issues that can be explored more deeply each time the topic is treated along the spiral approach. Otherwise they will complain that they are getting the same topics year after year, and they will quit paying attention. Presenting diverse current technological application contexts is a key way to help students stay engaged with the repeated ideas and satisfy the demand for relevance.

With the great demands on teachers' time, skills, and energy, they need extra help from the textbook. More help is needed for those teachers who, as often happens, end up teaching a new topic, or even a new subject, without adequate preparation. The teacher's edition (TE) is the usual answer to this dilemma.

Most TEs answer routine questions about how much time to spend on a given topic and what materials should be ordered. They also give the teacher suggestions for demonstrations, additional projects, and so on. Recently, TEs have been developed which address questions about children's naive conceptions: Two types will be presented here. One is a TE of a lab manual emphasizing the development of more student discretion in the laboratory, and the other is the TE of a text that can be used in the classroom to more effectively teach photosynthesis.

The science laboratory can be a particularly good place to diagnose, analyze, and attempt to correct naive conceptions of students, since the lab usually allows students more freedom for movement, more independent thought, and more casual conversation with the teacher. Yet such freedom is unlikely to happen if lab procedures are so highly structured that students only seek the accepted answers for filling in the blanks in rote fashion. To create a more meaningful learning experience in the laboratory, a procedure called Extending Discretion (ED) (Cavana and Leonard, 1985) has been devised that could be quite useful in changing the naive conceptions of students.

Using ED, the distinction is first made between prescribed tasks, (such as titration, microscope use, etc., where there is no choice of procedure) and discretionary tasks (where there is a choice in method, procedure, or material). If the lab is discretionary, the teacher considers how much time is needed for the complete exercise and how many steps are suggested. It may then be possible to reduce the number of tasks, thus allowing more time for each task. Individual students would be encouraged to work for longer periods than others who need more teacher help. Analyses of the Biological Sciences Curriculum Study (BSCS) Green Version and Chemistry in Experimental Science (CHEMS) in this study show that much greater discretionary time can be allowed in almost every experiment.

The results over three years show that some students can start with discretionary times of 15 minutes, then increase to two to three hours by the end of the year. Many can extend to two weeks. The 16-year-old students demonstrated a significantly greater understanding of laboratory concepts and produced a higher quality of laboratory reports. The researchers believe that these results arose from the students being required to think through the concepts more thoroughly from the beginning of the experiment. These results suggest that the ED approach could also be used to correct naive conceptions. Since students must think through and plan the experiment, they have to reconcile scientific theory, their own theory, and the similarities and differences between them. When a teacher is attentive to the kinds of naive conceptions typically held by students and is aware of approaches to pursue in order to correct these conceptions, there is a much better chance for correction. But how can there be time for all this? In the study, the authors found that teacher preparation time (set ups and instructions before labs) in the ED approach dropped to one-half because students learned to be more self-reliant.

TEs addressing naive science can also be helpful in the classroom. Using a modified classroom approach, two sequential studies from Michigan State provide an excellent illustration of how already existing material can be adapted to solve alternate conception problems. The first study (Smith, 1983) analyzed changes in fifth-grade students' conceptions about how green plants get their food. The instruction was based on chapters three to six of the Rand McNally SCIS "Communities" unit, which is organized around a "learning cycle" consisting of three phases: exploration, invention, and discovery. Since this cycle is designed to move students from naive preconceptions to more scientific concepts, SCIS is characterized as a conceptual-change strategy. The four-chapter sequence includes elements that were designed to expose naive conceptions and discrepant events. However, the results were poor. After instruction in bean-plant growth, only one student in the class appeared to hold the intended scientific conception, so the study then focused on "what went wrong?" Among the possible answers to this question were:
• Empirical ambiguity (e.g., generalizing from one or two cases)
• Ambiguity in discourse (e.g., embryo is both a part and a condition)
• Loose framing of important issues (e.g., no questions focusing on predictions about germination)
• Attacking the wrong preconception (e.g., notion that food is additive, so air and even light could be alternatives—one student thought that the bean plants would continue to grow in the dark because photosynthesis only required light, water, and air. Since the plant had two of these three, it should be able to do it.)

The second study (Roth, 1985) analyzed the previous results and reasons for error and developed a student text and a teacher guide as support materials for the lessons. The guide was developed to help teachers recognize students' naive conceptions and to help students give up these conceptions in favor of the scientific explanation of photosynthesis.

Technology. It has been argued in this paper that the pre-college curriculum should attack the students' naive conceptions while emphasizing fewer topics in greater depth ("less may be more") and in spiral fashion, a broader integration (of all subjects, but especially the sciences), and a greater extension (STS in a global context). While this is a very difficult goal to achieve, it may be more manageable with some of the techniques already mentioned, as well as with modern computer technology. Several examples of useful computer technology follow.

LOGO is worthy of consideration. Teachers who have used it in the classroom, from kindergarten upwards, usually agree with S. Papert (1980) that children often think differently, with more clarity, after using LOGO. Children, as well as adults, only need to construct a few triangles or houses before considering how angles are measured and fit together. Programs like Rocky's Boots and Robot Odyssey (Electronic Learning Co.) help children learn to think logically and to build their own complex devices that work only if the rules of logic are obeyed. Green Globs (Conduit) helps students learn to use algebraic equations to construct graphs. In physics, some programs provide routine physics textbook problems but will supply only information requested by the student. The difference is that the student must analyze the problem more deeply and then ask for information; it is not presented for simple insertion into little-understood formulas.

Microcomputer-based labs (MBLs) are even more useful for exploring topics in depth. Pioneered by the Technical Education Research Center (TERC), MBLs allow the student to acquire data in the laboratory through probes directly connected to the computer. Probes can be used to measure temperature, light, or sound and to produce graphic displays. Thus students can become involved immediately with very powerful measuring devices, akin to those of a research lab. Recent research also suggests that naive conceptions can be quickly and easily challenged and possibly corrected if graphs, such as the kind microcomputers can quickly produce, are displayed immediately for the students' consideration (Brasell, 1987). MBLs are also useful in the problem-solving format suggested earlier. With STS as a curriculum organizer, students use MBL probes in the study of acid rain, which could lead to an integration of biology with chemistry and of environmental studies with social studies. (See, e.g., National Geographic Kids Network Acid Rain Project.)

Most of the early research on alternative conceptions focuses on the physics of motion as an area of simple structure—with many tenacious alternate concepts. Some recent work involving microworlds (interactive simulations) seems quite promising in combatting naive conceptions. B. White and P. Horowitz (1987) used computer simulation to create microworlds whose properties students could investigate. This was part of an attempt to reduce the gap between the world of science and students' understanding. Students were given several laws for each microworld and asked to determine the correct laws and to determine which ones are better than others.

There were four distinct phases within each microworld:
1. Motivation—make predictions based on real-world ideas.
2. Model Evolution—solve problems and perform experiments in the context of the computer microworld.
3. Formalization—evaluate a set of laws and from the correct ones choose the better laws based on precision, generality, and simplicity.

4. Transfer—compare answers from laws with answers from phase one and devise experiments to test the laws.

As noted earlier, two classes of physics-naive sixth graders exposed to instruction based on these tenets performed better on a set of classic force and motion problems than other physics-naive sixth graders or high-school physics students.

These results provide evidence to support the belief that concepts formerly considered much too difficult and abstract for the elementary-school student can be reformulated and recast into effective procedures.

All of the examples of this section emphasize that three major factors have to be considered in instruction:
• the form and content of the students' mental models
• how to represent the phenomena to be understood
• the number and kind of instructional activities needed to produce change or development of principles and strategies

Summary

This paper has attempted to analyze three aspects of science curriculum in the United States—as intended, as implemented, and as achieved. From the general needs of our democratic society, the educational goal of critical thinking emerged, as paramount and closely connected with every aspect of scientific literacy. National committees have recently asserted that science is intimately connected to both technology and society, and all three should be a feature of the curriculum. The world's recent disasters have emphasized not only this STS connection but established the global context of energy and environment issues. The cognitive implications are enormous, and there is a great need for research that will lead to effective designs for bridging the gap between the intended and learned curriculum.

The dynamic, human, and revolutionary aspects of science have too often been buried beneath the mere cataloging of facts, theories, and laws, and it needs to reemerge. What big ideas of science should be emphasized? Perhaps those that are the nation's and world's biggest problems. Whatever ideas are chosen should reflect valid science, be fruitful, meaningful, and pervasive in a variety of STS contexts. Certainly they should be connected with students' inquiry and experiences in the classroom. Certainly they should make it clear to all that searching in depth for big solutions will integrate the sciences with the humanities.

From cognitive research comes the added awareness of what already makes sense to the student—naive science. If these concepts are to be replaced by valid scientific ones, perhaps the curriculum needs restructuring not only in terms of what idea builds on what, but how often the ideas need to be introduced in a variety of contexts. This suggests a spiral approach that can be easily adopted in our lower grades.

Finally, to implement the above ideas, we must give our teachers better training and better support. The training should focus on the students' naive science concepts in terms of awareness and conceptualization, then ways of using this focus in the classroom. The support would come from newer technologies and a better kind of textbook. The text should be an aid to the student, viewed as a guide to a changing world.

References

Brasell, H. (1987). The effect of real-time laboratory graphing on learning graphic representations of distance and velocity. *Journal of Research in Science Teaching, 24*(4), 385.

Bush, V. (1946). Endless horizons. Washington, DC: Public Affairs Press.

Cavana, G. R., and Leonard, W. H. (1985). Extending discretion in high school science curricula. *Science Education, 69*(5), 593.

Champagne, A., Gunstone, R., and Klopfer, L. (1985). Effecting changes in cognitive structures among physics students. In L. H. T. West and A. L. Pines (Eds.), *Cognitive structure and conceptual change.* (p. 163). New York: Academic Press.

Conant, J. B. (1951). *Science and common sense* (p. 24). New Haven: Yale University Press.

Di Sessa, A. (1987). The third revolution in computers and education. *Journal of Research in Science Teaching, 24*(4), 343.

Di Sessa, A., Gilbert, J. K., and Swift, D. J. (1985). Towards a Lakatosian analysis of the Piagetian and alternative conceptions research programs. *Science Education, 69*(5), 681.

Driver, R., Guesne, E., and Tiberghien, A. (1985). *Children's ideas in science.* Philadelphia: Milton Keynes.

Gabel, D., Samuel, K., Helgeson, S., McGuire, S., Novak, J., and Butzow, J. (1987). Science education research interests of elementary teachers. *Journal of Research in Science Teaching, 24*(7), 659.

Hamrick, L., and Harty, H. Influence of resequencing general science content on the science achievement, attitudes toward science, and interest in science of sixth grade students. *Journal of Research in Science Teaching, 24*(1), 15.

Harms, N. C. and Yager, R. E. (1981). *What research says to the science teacher.* (Vol. 3). Washington, DC: National Science Teachers Association.

Helgeson, S. L., Blosser, P. E., and Howe, R. W. (1977). *The status of precollege science, mathematics, and social science education: 1955–1975.* (Vol. 1). Columbus, OH: Center for Science and Mathematics Education, Ohio State University.

Hirsch, E. D. (1987). *Cultural literacy: What every American needs to know.* Boston: Houghton Mifflin.

Holton, G., and Roller, D. H. (1958). *Foundations of modern physical science.* (p. 232). San Francisco: Addison Wesley.

Kuhn, T. (1962). *The structure of scientific revolutions.* Chicago: Chicago University Press.

Lansdown, B., Blackwood, R. E. and Brandwein, P. F. (1972). *Teaching elementary science through investigation and colloquium.* New York: Harcourt Brace Javonovich.

Lawrenz, F. (1986). Misconceptions of physical science concepts among elementary school teachers. *School Science and Mathematics, 86*(8), 653.

Lederman, L. (1987). Science and technology policies and priorities: a comparative analysis. *Science, 237,* 1125.

Medawar, P. B. (1963, September 12). *The Listener.* (p. 337), BBC Publications.

National Science Board Commission. (1983). *Educating Americans for the 21st century.* Washington, DC: National Science Foundation.

National Science Teachers Association. (1985). *Science-Technology-Society: Science education for the 1980s.* Washington, DC: National Science Teachers Association.

Osborne, R., and Freyberg, P. (Eds.). (1985). *Learning in Science.* London: Heinemann.

Papert, S. (1980). *Mindstorms.* New York: Basic Books.

Piaget, J. (1929). *The child's conception of the world.* London: Routledge and Kegan Paul.

Popper, K. (1965). *The logic of scientific discovery.* New York: Harper and Row.

Rosenthal, D. B. (1983). Science and society in high school biology textbooks: 1963–1983. *Dissertation Abstracts International 44,* 1747-A. Rochester, New York: University of Rochester.

Roth, K. (1985). *Food for plants: Teacher's guide.* Michigan State University, ED 256 624.

Shamos, M. (1988). The lesson every child need not learn. *The Sciences, 28*(4), 14.

Smith, E. (1983). *Teaching for conceptual change; Some ways of going wrong.* Michigan State University, ED 237 493.

Stake, R. E., and Easley, J. A. (1978). *Case studies in science education.* Urbana, Illinois: Center for Instructional Research and Curriculum Evaluation, University of Illinois.

Staver, J. R., and Bay, M. (1987). Analysis of the project synthesis goal cluster orientation and inquiry emphasis of elementary science textbooks. *Journal of Research in Science Teaching, 24*(7), 629.

Weiss, I. R. (1978). *Report of the 1977 national survey of science, mathematics, and social studies education.* Research Triangle Park, North Carolina: Center for Educational Research and Evaluation, Research Triangle Institute.

Weiss, I. R. (1987). The 1985–86 National Survey of Science and Mathematics Education. In A. Champagne and L. Hornig (Eds.), *The science curriculum.* Washington, DC: American Association for the Advancement of Science.

West, L. H. T., and Pines, A. L., (Eds.). (1985). *Cognitive structure and conceptual change.* New York: Academic Press.

White, B., and Horwitz, P. (1987). *Thinker tools: Enabling children to understand physical laws.* BBN Laboratories, Inc. Report # 6470. Cambridge, Massachusetts.

Wittrock, M. C. (1974). Learning as a generative process. *Educational Psychology, 111,* 87.

Visual Literacy in Science Textbooks

Robert V. Blystone
Trinity University
San Antonio, Texas
Beverly C. Dettling
Trinity University
San Antonio, Texas

"Beware of pretty pictures . . . for they may lead one astray! Attractiveness is one thing; usefulness, another."

—P. C. Duchastel

P. C. Duchastel in very few words calls attention to the role of pictures in textbooks. Few users of textbooks, instructor and student alike, are literate enough to derive full value from the textbook's illustrations. As textbooks increase in length at all grade levels, they are becoming more pictorial. Illustrations are assuming a more dominant role in the message of the textbook. While written text evaluation is quite complete, few guidelines exist for the evaluation of the pictorial information. Many authors and publishers do not incorporate the illustrations with the text as well as they should. This paper will review recent information as it pertains to the important topic of visual literacy in science textbooks.

This paper is intended to aid the science teacher who has limited time and opportunity to review the literature on educational topics. This is not an exhaustive review of the illustration literature but rather a sampling of that literature. The intent of this work is to show how illustrations can affect the classroom performance of science students. Also, information is given to assist in analyzing the quality and type of textbook illustrations. The final objective of this work is to introduce the idea that visual literacy is an important skill. A broad sample of references is included to allow the reader to pursue the topic further.

The Changing Science Textbook

J. Doblin (1980) estimates that 85 percent of all the messages we receive are visual in nature. He continues by dividing visual messages into two types: "orthography (writing words according to standard usage) and iconography (representations by pictures or diagrams)." Doblin calls attention to the fact that prose is also a part of the visual medium along with illustrations. In this report we will deal with iconography, or in simpler terms, illustration. The use of the term illustration will be in its broadest sense: that of a non-prose device. Included in this usage would be artwork of all types: graphs, charts, flowcharts, diagrams, line drawings, pictures, photographs, and symbols.

An overview of developments in the evolution of illustrations in American textbooks is found in P. Mulcahy and S. J. Samuels' (1987) review. They observe that in the mid-nineteenth century, illustrations began to accompany content area materials, especially in geography. Mulcahy and Samuels traced illustrations as they became more of a comprehension aid "as American educational methods changed from a rote-learning method of instruction to one that involved using the five senses to acquire and remember information." P. P. Lynch and P. D. Strube (1985) provide a different perspective with their review of the history of the last 100 years of the science textbook. They follow the progression in the change of authorship of the science textbook: "Over a period which has seen the author of science texts change from clergymen to scientists to teachers to committees, there has been something of a narrowing rhetorical style." By narrowing of rhetorical style, Lynch and Strube refer to the change in focus toward descriptive science and away from the integration of science into life as a whole: "The modern textbook is often very weak in regard to integration of knowledge and it is not surprising to find a somewhat flat interpretation of ideas, often lacking in terms of values or any appreciative dimension." Both reviews indicate that the textbook had changed over the period of a century. On the one hand, science books now incorporate instructive pictures, while on the other, they have narrowed their focus. Using Doblin's terminology, the iconographic role of the textbook has increased while the rhetorical range of the orthographic aspect of the textbook has narrowed.

The amount of illustration use has increased in the last several decades. R. V. Blystone and K. Barnard (1988) surveyed college introductory biology textbooks published between 1950 to 1984. They found that recent books have nearly 300 percent more photographs and twice as many graphic representations than books published 35 years ago (after adjusting for differing lengths of books). An upper-level college biology textbook now typically has as many as 1,500 pieces of art with all charts, graphs, and line drawings in color. Blystone and Barnard further note that the increase in biology textbook length was associated more with additional illustrations and less with additional text. The increase in the number of illustrations is reflected in all science textbooks at both secondary-school and college levels.

Duchastel and R. Waller (1979) observe that "there is, of course, great variability across subject matters in the attitudes adopted toward illustrations: in some areas, such as medicine, science, and technology, illustrations and diagrams are more often recognized as an essential part of the presentation: whereas areas such as the humanities, education, and the social sciences have a basically literary tradition." It comes as no surprise that science textbooks in such subjects as college biology would have 1,500 pieces of artwork. However, B. D. Smith and J. M. Elifson (1986) report that even college history textbooks have had a 40-fold increase in the number of illustrations during a 20-year period from 1960 to 1980.

The role of illustrations in textbooks is expanding in all disciplines, yet problems exist. Doblin (1980) summarizes the difficulty.

> Only professional artists, designers, or architects are taught to use iconography fluently as language. The vast majority are taught only the three R's, which comprise only one of the two major forms of communication. The result is that most people fail to develop half their ability to communicate, think, and solve problems. As Joseph Albers is reputed to have said: "One in a hundred thinks, one in a thousand sees." Iconographic language can be structured and taught but, until it is, the public will remain half illiterate.

Visual literacy is a real issue both in the classroom and in the textbook. We are expanding the visual information base; however, if that base is to have the desired cognitive effect, we must expand our visual literacy.

The Scope of the Problem

The textbook represents the most identifiable educational tool that a science teacher possesses. Virtually every science course employs the use of a textbook. P. Goldstein (1978) estimates that 75 percent of classroom time and 90 percent of homework time involves textbook use. The textbook market in the United States has an annual expenditure of more than one-and-a-half billion dollars (Apple, 1984). Each year for just college introductory biology, more than 400,000 textbooks are sold (Blystone, 1987b). The number of science textbooks produced and the dollar volume expended on them is quite large. Incorporation of textbooks into the teaching strategy is extensive.

With such a robust market and need for science textbooks, why are so many comments of concern, criticism, and complaint heard? Titles of four recent papers exemplify the perceptions of many about science textbooks: (1) "What high school chemistry texts do well and what they do poorly," D. L. Gabel, 1983; (2) "Are they 'dumbing down' the textbooks?" E. B. Fiske, 1984; (3) "Better textbooks? Dim outlook ahead," B. DeSilva, 1986; and (4) "Middle school science texts: What's wrong that could be made right?" A. Champagne, 1987. These articles echo the concern expressed by many that textbooks need considerable improvement in spite of the resources expended to produce them.

As textbooks receive widespread criticism, the value of their illustrations is often downplayed. For example, M. J. Davies, editor and publisher of the *Harfort Currant*, says that poor textbook quality exists because "examination of schoolbooks by selection committees is often cursory, and decisions sometimes are based on such irrelevant criteria as *illustrations* (emphasis added), price or personality of sales agents" (Davies, 1986). Similarly H. Tyson-Berstein, textbook consultant for the Council of Chief State School Officers and for the Rand Corporation, refers to illustrations in the list of "mundane questions" that educators "must wrestle with." She continues by blaming poor textbook quality on the committee members' practices such as "making decisions on the basis of the extras, the *pictures* (emphasis added), or the conveniences of the teacher's guide" (Tyson-Berstein, 1987). Many textbook critics consider illustrations an irrelevant criteria upon which to base textbook selection.

Other textbook critics simply overlook the instructional function of illustrations and focus solely on the quality of prose. For example, DeSilva (1986) does not include the instructional quality of illustration in his list of key aspects of textbooks. Far too many people consider textbook illustrations as window decoration whose purpose is to produce sales. Critics have analyzed the accuracy, clarity, and appropriateness of the prose for student cognitive level and experience; but far too often, the critics do not analyze the textbook illustrations for these same qualities. Duchastel (1978) sums up this problem with the following statement: "Rarely are illustrations in text ever considered as important instructional variables."

The first step toward improved visual literacy is a recognition by all concerned of the importance of illustration to the message of the book. Critics, authors, and teachers must take into account the role of the visual image in student comprehension of textbook material. The scope of problems with textbook illustration is demonstrated below with three examples supported by Figures 1 through 3. These three examples represent some of the problems associated with visual literacy:

- text-illustration conflict
- variability of illustration content
- complexity of illustration

Figure 1 relates the problem where text and illustration do not coincide. Blystone (1987a) reports that all high-school biology textbooks in print in

1984 incorrectly represented information concerning cell structure: The nuclear envelope is incorrectly labeled as the nuclear membrane. These illustrations show two membranes forming an envelope, but the label and the text refer to a single nuclear membrane. Such a text-illustration conflict could lead to confusion on the part of the student. This example reinforces E. Marek's (1986) conclusion that student misconceptions in biology may rest in large measure on the book that the student uses.

Figure 1

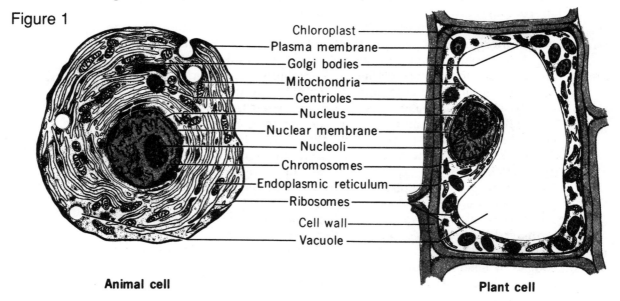

Animal cell   **Plant cell**

From BSCS *Biological Science: An Inquiry into Life*, 4th ed., 1980, Figure 3-17, (p. 90). Copyright 1980 by Biological Sciences Curriculum Study. Reprinted by permission.

Blystone became aware of the nuclear envelope problem in high-school texts through his participation in the Advanced Placement Program in Biology. While reading the 1984 essay question on plant cell structure, he found that three quarters of the students who identified the nuclear boundary did so with the term "nuclear membrane." These students were using college texts for their AP courses rather than high-school texts. Even though almost all college texts, with one exception in 1984, identified their nuclear boundaries with the term nuclear envelope, the students still used the term "nuclear membrane." Blystone concluded that students may have retained their first impression learning from their high-school text or that their AP teachers, who often live in two teaching worlds—regular biology and AP biology, used the terminology found in the more frequently used high-school texts. In this specific instance, the high-school texts were clearly out-of-date.

The nuclear boundary example of text-illustration conflict does offer one favorable relationship between the text and the illustration; the text does refer to the illustration, although incorrectly. Too frequently there is little interplay between the text and the illustration. As discussed later, the two are often developed independently when the textbook is produced. This dichotomy of book development can lead to problems like the nuclear boundary issue.

The second example of an illustration problem in textbooks considers the variation in illustration content dealing with the same topic. Textbook publishers clearly want to be up-to-date when they produce a science textbook at any grade level. Yet, the development of illustrations for textbooks does not present the cognitive sophistication found in the development of the text prose. Publishers apply numerous readability measures and general interest measures to textbook prose (for example, Dale and Chall, 1958; Fry, 1977; and Flesch, 1948). In fact, microcomputer programs have now been

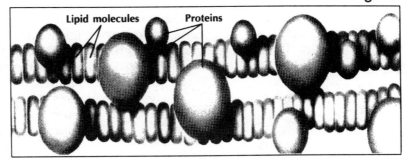

developed to analyze
reading level and
grammatical structure
as one writes. In regard
to illustration, however,
the measure of the
illustration's effective-
ness and its readability
is less precise. Consider
the different approaches
in Figure 2's illustra-
tions of the fluid mosaic
model of membrane
structure.

From *Biology: Living Systems*, 4th ed., (p. 75), by R. F. Oram, 1983, Columbus, OH: Charles E. Merrill. Copyright 1983 by Merrill. Reprinted by permission.

The five books represented by the illustrations in Figure 2 are all oriented toward high-school students of the same ability. All five texts have a reading

Figure 2b

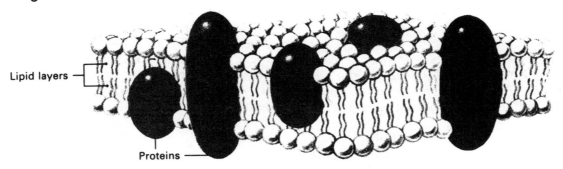

From *Biology*, (p. 102), by H. D. Goodman, T. C. Emmel, L. E. Graham, F. M. Slowiczek, and Y. Schechter, 1986, Orlando, FL: Harcourt, Brace, Jovanovich. Copyright 1986 by Harcourt, Brace, Jovanovich. Reprinted by permission.

difficulty level within two grade levels of each other. (See Walker, 1980, for a study showing how similar reading levels are for competing textbooks.) The level of illustration difficulty, however, differs more than two grade levels.

A comparison of the five illustrations reveals the following points. All five membrane models use at least two colors in their representations. The

Figure 2c

range of information
conveyed varies
significantly between
them. Four indicate
that the lipid bilayer
has molecules with
long-chained fatty
acids (not by name).
Four illustrations
depict the model in
three dimensions,
although one (Figure
2a) does not integrate
the proteins into the
lipid bilayer. Three
provide a "smooth"
molecular view, while
two (Figures 2d, 2e)
use a "stick" molecular

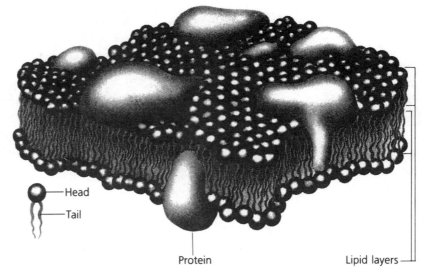

From *Modern Biology*, (p. 67), by A. Towle, 1989, Austin, TX: Holt, Rinehart & Winston. Copyright 1989 by Holt, Rinehart & Winston. Reprinted by permission.

view. One model gives proteins shape and functional form (Figure 2e); another model indicates membrane asymmetry (Figure 2d). Clearly, Figure 2a conveys the least scientific information. Figure 2c is perhaps the most scientifically artistic, although the "jellybean" nature of Figure 2b makes it memorable. Figures 2d and 2e are the most content ambitious with Figure 2e hinting at membrane transport phenomena.

The range of information content and misinformation content in Figure 2 demonstrates the extent of the problem with illustrations in science textbooks. The visual-comprehension level reads both well below and above the intended tenth-grade level audience. In our estimation Figure 2c represents grade 10 comprehension and use. Figure 2a is perhaps middle-school level, and 2e would be worthy of introductory college. The other two figures fall in between these extremes. Even though this entire set of illustrations should address a tenth-grade level, the illustrations reflect a difference of six grade levels.

Figure 2d

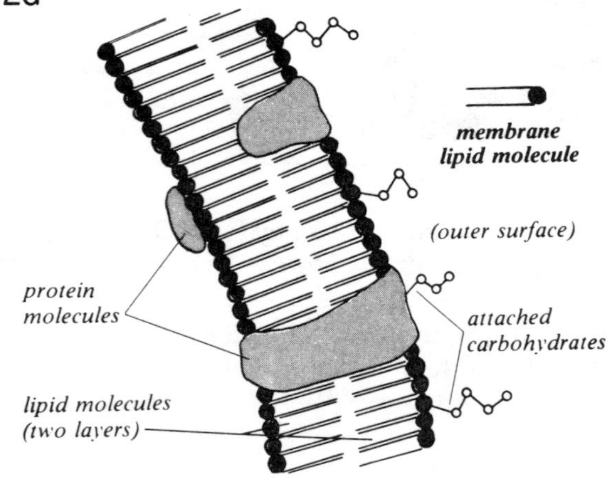

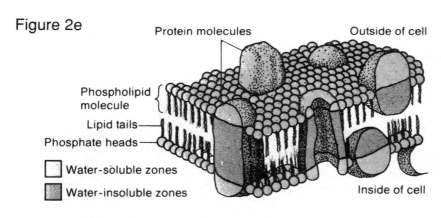

From *Biological Science: A Molecular Approach*, Blue Verson, Fifth ed., (p. 128, figure 6-12), by Toby Klang (Ed.), 1985, Lexington, MA: D. C. Heath and Company. Copyright 1985 by D. C. Heath and Company. Reprinted by permission.

This kind of variation in illustration-content levels is found, not only in comparisons between textbooks, but within the same textbook. Textbook editors are very careful to keep the prose on grade level throughout the book, but the same is not true for illustrations. At the author-publisher level, illustrations are not consistently developed for the textbook.

At the teacher level, textbook illustrations can quickly challenge the instructor's content knowledge. The content-rich Figure 2e shows a protein pore. How many teachers would realize that the central interior of this protein molecule is incorrectly labeled as a water-insoluble zone? Although this example is of an illustration error, how many Biology I teachers would have appreciated a correct illustration? Content-ambitious illustrations in high-school level science textbooks can often exceed the level of content presentation in the text prose. The variation in age range of illustration content is a very serious problem in textbook design.

Figure 2e

From *Heath Biology*, (p 102), by J. E. McLaren and L. Rotundo, 1985, Lexington, MA: D. C. Heath and Company. Copyright 1985 by D. C. Heath & Company

The third example deals with the complexity of an illustration. Figure 3 is from a junior-level college cell biology text and is an appropriate illustration for the grade level. As simple as the figure may appear, it represents seven distinct time periods and at least 13 discrete events. Such complexity and information denseness in an illustration raises new pedagogical problems.

Figure 3

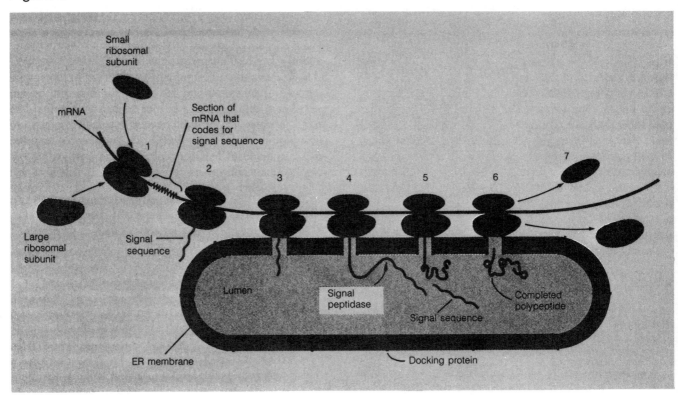

This figure is from *The World of Cells*, (p. 329), by W. Becker, 1986, Palo Alto, CA: Benjamin/Cummings. This figure is in turn based upon a figure from *The Journal of Cell Biology*, 1975, vol. 67, p. 835, by copyright permission of the Rockefeller University Press. Permission also granted by G. Blobel and B. Dobberstein.

How many instructors take into account the complexity of such illustrations when making reading assignments? How many students take the time to work their way through such an illustration as Figure 3 as they read their textbook? Many, students and teachers alike, do not realize the time investment needed to probe the content of an illustration such as Figure 3. To further complicate the issue, information about how students interact with textbook illustrations is quite limited, and much of the existing literature concerns elementary grades and nonscience topics. We have a poor information base on how students extract information from illustrations of science material.

These three examples indicate that from the vantage of authors, teachers, and students, the literate use of illustrations in science textbooks is far from perfect. Text-illustration agreement, variation in range of presentation, and cognitive complexity are but three problems among many. Now that we have an idea of the scope of the problems, what do we really know about illustrations?

Awareness of the Functional Role of Illustrations

E. B. Bernhardt (1987) observes that "texts are perceived as holding truths or facts. Their function is to bring these truths or facts to students so that they may absorb them . . . that is, to reproduce the text." Bernhardt further argues that ". . . teachers need to perceive texts as participants—as agents with which students interact. . . . Teachers need to probe students' derived meanings from text." We would sharpen Bernhardt's words to include that teachers need to probe students' derived meanings from text prose and illustrations. All concerned in the textbook process must be aware of the growing importance of illustrations to the meaning of the book.

Chemistry textbooks have long reflected the value of certain forms of illustration. Symbolic illustration is commonly employed in chemistry books in the form of chemical reactions and molecular formulas. Organic ring structures are familiar to many in science. J. D. Herron (1983) comments on the use of chemical symbols: "These representations are familiar to chemistry teachers, but students must learn to use them and authors must teach students to interpret the symbols." Herron recognizes that students must be taught to interpret this form of illustration. In this case, symbolic illustration awareness is a part of the textbook process at all levels: author, teacher, editor, and student.

W. G. Holliday and colleagues have measured the effectiveness of labeled drawings in improving student comprehension in several areas of science. In a 1976 report, Holliday and D. A. Harvey show how drawings could significantly improve middle-school students' comprehension of such physical concepts as density, pressure, and Archimedes' Principle. Physics texts have long employed diagrams of such concepts as inclined planes and pulleys. With added arrows showing direction of movement or force, diagrams can help students visualize many more concepts. Again the author, teacher, and student have developed a rapport between this type of illustration and the comprehension of physics.

The functional role of illustrations in the curriculum is most easily identified in the form of graph reading. Beginning at the elementary-grade levels in reading and mathematics, students are taught skills associated with graphs. In the secondary curriculum, social studies and the sciences rely on graph-reading skills. With graphs so heavily used in the curriculum, it comes as no surprise that some of the best studies about the use of illustrations concern graphs.

B. V. Roller (1980) reports her findings about the graph-reading abilities of 13-year olds. She finds that students read graphs better when the graph is isolated and not embedded in the text. She agrees with "the hypothesis that text and graph information are not commonly merged in the mind of the reader." And upon interviewing students, she records that many students thought graphs increased the difficulty of reading. Many of the seventh-grade students also indicated that they depended on their teachers to explain the graphs. Roller further comments: "These seventh graders were very similar to first graders learning to read. They exhibited much of the behavior usually associated with beginning reading . . . including reading aloud, whispering, subvocalization, following lines of print with a forefinger, following grid and information lines with fingers. . . ." Could it be that learning to read illustrations follows learning to read text by as much as six years? Could a college student with on-grade level reading ability have a middle-school illustration comprehension level?

Following this line of questioning, D. Kauchak, P. Eggen, and S. Kirk (1978) provide additional information on learning from graphic materials in upper elementary science students. They concluded that it was harder to cue a reader dealing with a graph. (A cue is a device used to help focus the learner's attention.) They found that textual cues are more readily understood than graphic cues. Kauchak et al. speculated that "in reading a graph it is possible to jump from data to data, and data to axes." A student might jump over a graphic cue; whereas with linear text, it is harder to miss the cue.

Approaching graphs from the standpoint of how to construct them, J. Bertin (1980) offers these insights: ". . . one cannot look at a graph . . . as one looks at a painting or a traffic signal. One does not passively read a graph: one queries it." Bertin is persuasive in his position that "one must know how to ask useful questions" about a graph. As a graphmaker and cartographer, Bertin knows that a successful graph or map must make questions possible about the data portrayed in the illustration. Because an illustration adds this dimension of interpretation and questioning, it is harder to "read" than prose. Clearly, students have to be taught how to read an illustration; yet at the same time, it is harder to cue a student from within an illustration on how to read it.

In spite of the facts that illustrations are more difficult for students to comprehend, that they represent additional work for the instructor, and that they add time and cost for the author/designer/publisher; teachers prefer more illustrations in texts. In a sample of 640 biology teachers, D. L. Spiegel and J. D. Wright (1984) report that figures and diagrams placed first on a list of 21 text characteristics in terms of importance. Fourth on the list were charts, tables, and graphs; seventh was photographs; and tenth was color in graphic aids. Text characteristics such as chapter summaries, chapter objectives, and study questions at the beginning of the chapter were of less importance than the four visual elements listed. This preference for more illustrations by both teachers and students is borne out in other studies. For example, J. P. Barufaldi and R. J. Daily (1986) list "the use of pictures and diagrams to illustrate concepts or set-ups" as first in importance in a list of comprehension enhancers.

In contrast to teachers' growing awareness of the functional role of illustration, textbook-selection criteria continue to give illustrations a position of lesser importance. G. P. Redei (1984) and K. Berry and D. Lee (1982) describe features to consider when selecting science textbooks. Of 45 points in Redei's list, only two deal with illustrations and were 13th and 15th on his list. His illustration criteria call for "sufficient clear and self-explanatory illustrations" and "cheerful and pleasing appearance!" Berry and Lee list "visual aids" as the fifth of nine criteria for choosing textbooks. Textbook evaluators must give illustrations a more prominent position in the selection process.

Effectiveness of Illustrations

Why have textbook illustrations become a focus of attention in recent years? As late as 1978, J. L. Thomas drew the following conclusion concerning illustration use with fourth-grade science students: "The findings appear to indicate that the inclusion or exclusion of pictures in elementary science textbooks do not influence the comprehension of the material." Thomas' view reflects the opinions of the majority in the field through much of the 1970s. Today 95 percent of the pages of first-grade mathematics books and 60 percent of the pages of middle-school science books have illustrations on them (Evans, Watson, and Willows, 1987). As much as 50 percent of the cost of the production of a textbook can involve graphics according to John McClements (personal communication, Addison-Wesley, Menlo Park, CA). This change from an unfavorable view of illustrations to a favorable view occurred during the late 1970s.

Research by F. M. Dwyer and others uncovered a positive correlation in the use of certain illustrations and text-illustration combinations. Dwyer (1972) designed a controlled experiment in which he investigated an illustrated instruction sequence on the topic of the heart using a variety of graphic media. Through his use of photographs of the heart, photographs of models of the heart, and line drawings of the heart in black and white and in color, he determined that "all types of visuals are not equally effective in facilitating student achievement by different learning objectives." His statistical analysis revealed that students preferred color in diagrams. Other reports favoring the use of illustrations soon followed; for example, J. M. Royer and G. W. Cable's (1976) study concerning students' illustration-assisted learning about heat transfer, and Holliday's (1975) study of tenth-grade biology students learning from simple diagrams about plant hormones. Holliday disagreed with the negative correlation previous work on illustration had revealed and urged research and development people to stop "relying on intuition" and "explore techniques . . . which coincided more closely with theoretical requirements of learning." Therefore, in the late 70s, a better method for evaluating the effective use of illustrations was gradually developed.

Since methodology is so important in verifying the value of illustrations toward learning, the three papers described here in detail reveal several approaches to illustration methodology. Holliday, L. L. Brunner, and E. L. Donais (1977) studied the effect of flow diagrams on high-school biology students' learning, using the oxygen, carbon dioxide, nitrogen, and water cycles—37 concepts in all—as the teaching topic. They developed two types of flow diagrams: (a) a picture-word diagram in color and (b) a black and white blocked-word diagram. Both diagrams included all 37 concepts, and each diagram was accompanied by the same list of 22 instructive questions. Students were presented either the picture-word or blocked-word diagram instructional module. The students were advised to answer the accompanying 22 instructive questions in writing. Then they were given a 30-question multiple-choice post-test and a questionnaire. What makes this study unique, however, is that Holliday et al. divided their test students into low- and high-verbal-ability students. The low-verbal-ability students did significantly better on the post-test after using the picture-word diagram learning approach than the low-verbal-ability students using the block-word diagram sequence. High-verbal-ability students did about the same with either learning approach. Low-verbal-ability, picture-word diagram-trained students did almost as well as the high-verbal-ability, picture-word diagram-trained students on the post-test.

If the verbal ability of the sample had not been identified, the data collected would not have revealed any difference between picture-word diagram and block-word diagram learning. A conclusion can be drawn from this work: If high-verbal-ability students can perform at the same levels on either flow diagram, but low-verbal-ability students perform significantly better on picture-word diagrams, then textbook developers should favor picture-word diagrams which would allow the low-verbal-ability students to perform at their optimum.

In 1981, Holliday reported another approach to learning based on picture-word diagrams, again using biogeochemical cycles (oxygen, carbon dioxide, nitrogen, and water cycles). The effect of four learning protocols was studied on tenth-grade biology students that were carefully matched but randomly grouped: (a) picture-word diagram accompanied by 20 textbook study questions; (b) the same picture-word diagram accompanied by five sample questions; (c) the same picture-word diagram with no study questions; and (d) a prose passage describing the biogeochemical cycles in question. After a suitable study time, all four groups were given a 30-question multiple-choice exam. The study questions were carefully designed to reflect and elicit favorable responses for the post-test. On the post-test, students with the 20-question protocol and no-question protocol outperformed the 5-question and prose-protocol groups. Explanation of these data was that the 20-question students were thoroughly supported in their instruction. The no-question students had to devise their own study scheme, which apparently worked. The 5-question students were only partially cued to the subject matter by the few questions. They responded only to the five questions in their study and did not focus on other material not covered by the five questions. The prose-only group served as "controls." The conclusion to be drawn here by textbook developers is that picture-word diagrams should be supported completely—or not at all. Providing partial text support encourages the student to do poorly on illustration-based text.

D. A. Hayes and J. E. Readence (1983) examined the degree of recall from several levels of illustration-dependent text. First, they selected four different text passages that were accompanied by illustrations. The selected text passages represented four levels of illustration dependency: high, moderate, slight, and total independence from illustration. Seventh-grade students were divided into four sample groups. In a four-by-four matrix, the four student groups read four selections. Each of the four selections was prefaced by different conditions:

1. Students read text without illustrations or instructions.
2. Students read text with illustrations, but no instructions.
3. Students read text with illustrations and were told that illustrations would help them.
4. Students read text with no illustrations but were told to visualize the text because it would help them.

Condition 1 yielded the expected results that high-illustration-dependent text produced poor recall; whereas, low-illustration-dependent and illustration-independent text produced much higher recall. Condition 2 resulted in nearly equal recall across all four illustration-dependent categories. Condition 3 produced slightly better results in the high-illustration-dependent text. Condition 4 produced results similar to condition 1 with some minor deviations. The conclusion to be drawn from this complex experiment is that text designed for illustration works "to the extent that the text depends on illustrations." A textbook developer should be aware that text and illustration dependence should agree with one another. If, for example, a text is designed for one illustration-dependency level and for reasons of budget or space, the illustrations are cut, the text must be rewritten to reflect the change in illustration support for a specific dependency level.

J. Peeck (1987) comments that a major effect of illustrations on learning and retention may be their ability to encourage the reader to invest more time in the cognitive effort. This motivational aspect is very difficult to test. Peeck also reports research in which subjects record the first five things they remember about an illustrated passage read the week before. Many of the responses were directly related to the illustrations associated with the passage. These results bring to mind how the memory encodes information. Is there a preference for pictorial input over text input? Motivational aspects of illustrations and memory encoding of illustrations are but two new areas receiving a great deal of attention in new experimental designs. The research into the effectiveness of illustrations has matured a great deal over the last 20 years.

W. H. Levie (1987) provides an exceptional overview into the current state of scholasticism in illustration research in his review article in Houghton and Willow's *The Psychology of Illustration Volume 1*. In excerpts from his final comments section, Levie summarizes:

> It is clear that "research on pictures" is not a coherent field of inquiry. An aerial view of the picture research literature would look like a group of small topical (sic) islands with only a few connecting bridges in between. . . . Those doing picture research usually are allied to some field such as development psychology, perception communications, art education, or education psychology and tend to focus on the literature in their own traditional area. . . . Thus, most picture research is embedded within separate areas usually identified by the mental process evoked by stimuli rather than by surface-level features of the stimuli themselves. . . . Efforts toward a "psychology of pictorial learning" might also make picture research more accessible to practitioners who design instructional illustration . . . an additional approach that brings together data and ideas from separate contexts could contribute much to our understanding of this pervasive, versatile mode of communication.

Levie also provides a conceptual framework for viewing the field. His outline below provides an excellent overview of the research completed in illustration today. The number in parentheses after each outline entry represents the number of references associated with each topic in Levie's bibliography. Levie selected his references "on the basis of recentness, significance, and availability (dissertations, convention papers, and low-circulation journals are not cited)."

Picture Perception (6)

theoretical approaches to picture perception (21)
attention and scanning (40)
interpreting figures and pictorial cues (40)
perceiving global meaning (25)

Memory for Pictures (6)

memory models (25)
recognition memory (44)
recall (20)
other types of memory research (27)

Learning and Cognition (7)

acquisition of knowledge (48)
problem solving and visual thinking (26)
the acquisition of cognitive skills (32)
media research (39)

Affective Responses to Pictures

arousal and emotional impact (17)
preferences (22)
attitudes (25)
aesthetic responses (31)

Categorizing Illustrations

In some ways a good illustration resembles a prose paragraph. An illustration should have the same question asked of it as does the prose paragraph: What is its purpose? Perhaps the place to start when questioning what purpose an illustration serves is into what category does the illustration fit. Several authors provide models for the categorization of illustrations.

Duchastel (1980) has developed, according to function, a three-category model for illustrations: attentional, explicative, and retentional. The attentional illustration is one where the main purpose is to keep the reader interested in the text. Cartoons, portraits of well-known persons, and aesthetic settings can perform this function. The explicative illustration "directly assists comprehension by visually clarifying a point in the text." Graphs and diagrams are two types of explicative illustration. And third in Duchastel's list, the retentional illustration assists recall better than verbal expression alone. This type of illustration provides information, such as spatial detail, that verbal text has a difficult time portraying. Duchastel continues by explaining that these three types of illustrations can overlap each other in function; and when designing an illustration, the functional categories and their possible overlap should be considered.

Doblin (1980) provides a very comprehensive structure for nontextual messages. First, information is broken into three content types: "nominal, names or terms given for identification or classification; noumenal, conceived by reason, but not knowable through the senses; phenomenal, known through experience rather than thought or intuition." Doblin then constructs a nine member matrix of information messages. Of interest to this report are the following categories: the visual nominal, visual noumenal, and visual phenomenal. Visual nominal illustrations are visual words such as trademarks and road signs. Visual noumenal information would be charts and graphs. Visual phenomenal illustration is the visual representation of reality and includes drawing, photography, and model making.

Doblin relates these categories to a "ladder of abstraction." He considers charts and graphs quite abstract, photographs slightly realistic, and models as very realistic. Doblin argues that a visually literate person should be able to discern types of visual messages. He then carries visual information messages into the area of persuasion and stimulation. From this vantage, he develops a model of message flow. Doblin's categories of persuasive message flow fall clearly into the realm of contemporary advertising. Knowing these categories, one can understand how the message is being delivered. Textbook illustrations are messages that few people understand in the terms that Doblin has presented. By matching his categories to a textbook illustration, the value of that illustration can be quickly ascertained.

M. Twyman (1979) categorizes graphic language in greater detail than Doblin. He presents a matrix that has 28 members, and his article richly details each cell of the graphic language matrix. Twyman considers the teaching of graphic language with these thoughts:

> On the whole, however, it is true to say that children are not taught to read the wide range of graphic language they will be confronted with in later life. Still less of course are children taught to originate information in anything like the range of approaches to graphic language presented in the matrix.

With his matrix in mind, Twyman calls attention to the conflict between the linear presentation format of verbal text and the non-linear presentation style of pictures. He indicates that the linear and non-linear forms are being combined regularly now and asks, "What are the consequences of switching from one mode to another and one configuration to another on both eye movements and cognitive processes?"

Twyman (1985), in a later article, outlines the eight variable factors that are part of graphic language: purpose, information content, configuration, mode, means of production, resources, users, and circumstances of use. He argues that each of these variables must be carefully considered if a graphic is to work well. These variables should be kept in mind when reviewing a text-book's illustration layout. Twyman then compares illustrations using a contrasting scheme of either/or categories: generality versus particularity; observation-based versus concept-based; and synoptic versus discrete. When reviewing these either/or categories in Twyman's paper, one begins to realize that there is much to consider when looking at a picture. Twyman summarizes, "there are occasions when the 'grammar' of a drawing needs to be understood in very precise terms before it can be 'read' accurately." E. Goldsmith (1984, 1987) presents a simpler method of categorizing the utility of illustrations. Goldsmith developed a 12-cell illustration-analysis matrix after working with an adult-literacy campaign in the United Kingdom. Her matrix relates four visual factors with three levels of communication. Her visual factors include:

> *unity*, which refers to a single image; *location*, the spatial relationships between two or more images within a single picture—particularly insofar as it concerns pictorial depth; *emphasis*, the hierarchical relationships between images; and *text parallels*, the relationship between text and picture.

Goldsmith defines her three levels of communication as follows:

> *syntactic*, which does not assume any recognition or identification of images; *semantic*, which concerns the basic recognition of an image, not implying specialized knowledge; and *pragmatic*, which reminds those concerned that readers will differ in age, sex, education, culture, interest, needs and so on. (Goldsmith, 1987, p. 54)

Her model considers such things as color, position, size, isolation, complexity, tonal contrast, directionality, and implied motion. In her 1987 paper, Goldsmith provides detailed examples of how to read illustrations. She points out how people of different ages scan illustrations differently. Both her matrix and examples stress the importance of being visually literate both as a reader and as a teacher.

Placing an illustration into some categorization scheme, one quickly realizes that an illustration is much like a paragraph of prose. It has a story to tell and unique ways in which this story can reveal itself. The references cited provide several different examples of schemes with which illustrations can be catalogued. One's level of visual literacy is quickly revealed by trying to apply these cataloguing systems to favorite illustrations.

Designing Illustrations

Designing illustrations is a difficult task. H. E. Paine (1980), art director for *National Geographic*, outlines some of the problems that illustrators must overcome: "how to show motion, growth, the passage of time, comparative scale, and how to see within." He presents these additional problems: "How much of a complex subject can be shown in one illustration or should it be divided into several parts? When should separate parts be synthesized? When do we depart from realism and do a schematic diagram?" He then speaks of how difficult it is to put labels into the art work. His article clearly calls attention to some of the problems that a graphic designer must solve.

W. D. Winn (1987) begins his article on illustration design by carefully defining each form of illustration.

> Graphs are taken to be those graphic forms that illustrate relationships among variables, at least one of which is continuous. . . . Charts are those graphic forms that illustrate relationships among categorical variables. . . . While the function of graphs and charts is to illustrate simple relationships among variables, the function of diagrams is to describe whole processes and structures often at levels of great complexity.

In each of the three illustration types defined, Winn determines the sequence and pattern of presentation in the space provided for the illustration. He concludes, ". . . the relative placement of elements in a chart, graph, or diagram and the devices, like lines, arrows, column headings, and boxes, are the core of visual argument." Winn always keeps comprehension at the heart of illustration design.

R. J. Levin, G. J. Anglin, and R. N. Carney (1987) provide ten commandments for picture facilitation (pp. 73–77). These humorously drawn commandments bear repeating.

Pictures shalt be judiciously applied to text, to remember it wholly.

Pictures shalt honor the text.

Pictures shalt not bear false fitness to the text.

Pictures shalt not be used in the presence of "heavenly" bodies of prose.

Pictures shalt not be used with text cravin' for images.

Pictures shalt not be prepared in vain.

Pictures shalt be faithfully created from generation to generation.

Pictures shalt not be adulterated.

Pictures shalt be appreciated for the art they art.

Pictures shalt be made to perform their appropriate functions.

For each of the commandments, Levin et al. provide substantive detail in a very carefully drafted article.

M. L. Fleming (1987) provides a list of principles which illustrations should address. His original article lists 25 principles which are keyed to illustrations in which the principles are employed. Below are listed 19 of the principles. Careful review of these principles reveals lessons useful for teaching in general as well as for the design of quality illustrations.

1. We can perceive at a glance . . . and store in immediate memory about seven familiar items.

2. Perceivers partition the available information. . . . They are said to chunk or cluster or group.

3. Where material to be learned is organized and that organization is apparent to the learner, acquisition will be facilitated.

4. The figural portion of a stimulus . . . is given more attention, is perceived as solid and well-defined, and appears to be in front of the ground.

5. Attention is drawn and held by complexity, providing the complexity does not exceed the perceivers' cognitive capacities.

6. Learning is facilitated where criterial cues are salient (dominant, apparent, conspicuous).

7. Learning to associate or relate two or more objects or events (stimuli and/or responses) is facilitated where they occur or are encountered in contiguity, that is, close together in time or space.

8. Where the beginning of a unit provides an introduction to the material which is relatively abstract and general, subsequent learning of related details within the unit can be facilitated.

9. A moderate degree of uncertainty or anxiety provides a strong incentive to act, that is, to attend carefully, to learn, to resolve the problem.

10. Objects and events encountered in proximity with each other, that is, close together in time or space . . . will tend to be perceived as somehow related. Comparisons will be facilitated, both similarities and differences becoming more apparent.

11. Perception is very selective. We attend to only a few of the sights, sounds, and smells available . . . in our environment.

12. Objects and events perceived as similar, in any of a number of ways such as appearance, function, quantity, direction, and structure, will tend to be grouped or organized together in perception.

13. Objects and events perceived as different, as standing in contrast along one or more dimensions, will tend to be . . . separately grouped.

14. Differences can be maximized by exaggerating the criterial features . . . and by eliminating or reducing the dominance of the non-criterial features.

15. The more concrete the things to be associated, the more readily they are learned and remembered. . . . More specifically, objects and pictures of objects are better remembered than their names.

16. In general, where the learner reacts to or interacts with the criterial stimulus, learning is facilitated. . . .

17. If a concept is basically spatial, like mountain, mile, cube, anatomy, leaf shape, Big Dipper, or Venus de Milo, then vision is appropriate.

18. Perception is strongly affected by what we expect or are "set" to perceive. This influences both what we select and how we organize and interpret it.

19. . . . [A]ttention is drawn to what is novel, to whatever stands in contrast to immediate past experience or to life-long experience.

Fleming provides concrete examples of artwork to substantiate the principles.

The design of illustrations has been primarily an intuitive action on the part of the graphic designer. Often the graphic artist works independently of the author of the text, and too frequently, the artist is not an expert in the subject matter being illustrated. M. A. Evans, C. Watson, and D. M. Willows (1987) reviewed the process by saying, "It is left to the illustrator(s) of the book, acting on the instructions of the designer or art director, to provide the exact composition and style of the illustrations. . . . Rarely, if ever, do authors and illustrators meet." However, new equipment is now being employed to determine the way a viewer looks at a piece of artwork. G. M. Schumacher and Waller (1985) describe machines that can follow the micro- and macro-movements of the eyes. By determining the way a reader studies a particular illustration, the illustration can be designed to gain the maximum response from the reader. Technology is aiding the graphic artist by giving the artist feedback as to what the reader finds interesting in the art work. Unfortunately, most publishers do not have the time or money to employ these new techniques extensively.

Similar attention is being given to the look of prose. J. J. Foster (1979) describes work where the look of the text is being examined. Such things as fonts, selective use of bold face type, and how the text is grouped or "chunked" impact on how the reader deals with the text. Printed text taken as a whole is, in a manner of speaking, an illustration. Considering chunked text as an illustration gives a new dimension to the problem of graphic design. Microcomputers and desktop publishing are calling increased attention to the look of the text.

Graphic design is a very specialized field, and the papers cited in this section provide an introduction to this literature. The visually literate person needs to appreciate the way graphic art is put together. This knowledge allows for selection of better artwork in textbooks and in its interpretation.

Improving Illustrations in Textbooks

Examination of textbooks reveals a great range of variation in illustration quality among books and even within the same textbook. With an art program contributing perhaps half the cost of the development of the textbook, one might argue that the money is not being wisely spent because of this uneven quality of illustration. How can science textbook illustrations be improved? Most sources point first at the publisher.

J. D. McInerney (1986) states: "Those who follow the publishing industry closely are convinced that the trend toward safe, in-house books will continue, because there is no inducement for publishers to change their current approach to textbooks." H. O'Donnell (1985), in reviewing the literature on improving textbooks, also indicates that publishers are reticent to make big changes in textbooks because of the big financial risks. More than ten years ago, M. Bowler (1978) charged that "publishers have been conditioned to believe that one of the secrets of success is to make textbooks, and especially the teacher's manual, simple and easy to follow—day-by-day and hour-by-hour." Finally, J. H. Osborn, B. F. Jones, and M. Stein (1985) state: "Our observation is that graphics in texts are almost always attractive; however, we suspect that they may not always be functional and that they occasionally overwhelm and distract from the text." All these reports indicate that textbook changes are necessary, but publishers are resisting such change.

The problem of textbook change goes beyond the publishers, however. H. Talmage (1986) believes that "three distinct types of expertise go into bringing 'good' materials to . . . students." She suggests that three groups are represented in the process: publisher, author, and teachers. Talmage places responsibilities on the teachers to hasten changes in textbooks. McInerney (1986), likewise, charges the teachers with responsibilities in the textbook-improvement process, indicating that teachers have an obligation to convey needed changes to the textbook publishers as well as to administrators.

A proportion of the responsibility rests with teachers to initiate changes in things such as better textbook illustrations. In fact, teachers represent the first step in the improvement process. However, an immediate difficulty is encountered; many teachers have little knowledge of textbook design, let alone the visual literacy needed to suggest changes in textbook graphics. Much of the motivation for producing this article rests with providing teachers an information resource for addressing the illustration problems of textbooks.

P. J. Thompson (1984) provides a concise source of information describing the way textbooks are organized and developed. She divides a textbook into five distinct parts: text matrix, text apparatus, illustration program, access features, and display elements. The text matrix is the actual written instructional material. The text apparatus is specially prepared pedagogical material used to deliver the instructional material. Access features include such things as the table of contents, headings, and index. Display elements are an intimate part of the textbook product package and include the book cover and chapter openings. The illustration program covers art, photos, and graphics used in the text. With so many parts and pieces to a textbook, the book is actually more frequently "assembled" rather than written. Thompson further argues that a textbook should be specifically researched for its own sake rather than as part of a reading program.

One conclusion to be drawn is that the major thrust for the improvement of textbook illustration rests with the teacher. It is the teacher who must discern whether the student understands the artwork in the textbook. It is the teacher who must determine whether the illustrations make any sense. To do this, the teacher must be visually literate. Once a teacher understands how well or poorly the illustration program works for a textbook, she/he must communicate the effectiveness of that program with the publisher. Improvement will come when an informed user has dialogue with the producer.

Illustrations in the Classroom

Illustrations must be used more effectively in student learning. What measures can be used to facilitate this objective? C. Gwyn (1987) outlines his structured approach for encouraging high-school physics students to read their textbooks more productively. His approach includes "reading aloud, outlining, and brainstorming." Extending Gwyn's principle of active textbook interaction, T. E. Scruggs and M. A. Mastropieri (1985) encourage their students to develop illustrations representing the material studied. They also suggest that the teacher preface the reading with an instructor-created illustration developed in the classroom. Similarly, K. P. Szlichcinski (1980) asks subjects to develop diagrams showing how certain equipment was operated. By analyzing the different drawings, Szlichcinski gains insight into the various ways the subjects viewed the operation of the equipment. K. L. Alesandrini and J. W. Rigney (1981) refer to this technique of student-produced illustrations of text as an "induced picture strategy." They also cite work indicating that "imposed pictures" (ones prepared for the student) were far more effective in science learning than the induced picture. The research on the effectiveness of student produced diagrams on learning is obviously mixed.

There is evidence that students do not actively manipulate the subject material as they read. J. H. Wandersee (1988), in his survey of college science students, includes a question asking whether students constructed their own charts, outlines, or diagrams as they read a new chapter. Of the sample of 133 students representing four college grade levels, 55 percent indicated they seldom employed such a reading technique. Of those that constructed tools, 65 percent made outlines, 10 percent lists, 9 percent diagrams, 6 percent charts, and 10 percent combinations. This study indicates that few students try to build visual aids of their own as they read. Therefore, it is all the more important that the suggestions of Gwyn, Scruggs and Mastropieri, and Szlichcinski be given consideration.

What can a teacher do to bring knowledge of the utility of illustrations into a more productive position in the classroom? Several ideas are offered here. Blystone (unpublished observation) has found the following exercise to be very useful in developing cell-structure concepts with college students after they had read their texts on the subject. Students recreate an optical slice through a "typical" cell. If a liver cell was magnified 10,000X and then viewed in an electron microscope, the area seen would be nearly equivalent to a piece of 8 1/2 x 11 inch paper. Based on what a student draws on the paper, it becomes quite evident whether the student understands the structural relationships of the cell. Thus, having a student visualize pictorially by drawing a concept on paper, the instructor can quickly gauge the progress of the student's understanding. We are suggesting that an induced picture strategy offers teachers an interesting possibility in learning situations. Blystone in an unpublished observation has also tried a reverse approach to illustration-dependent learning. His college-level students wrote a verbal translation of Figure 3 which was exceptional in the density of its information content. Most students required not less than three typewritten pages to accomplish this task. Students found that having to put a complex illustration back into words caused them to reevaluate the content of the text again. This exercise was most successful. In richly illustrated texts, it is important that an instructor determine the information density of the illustrations associated with a reading assignment. It is possible that a reading passage with only 10 pages may take far longer to comprehend than one with 30 pages because the short passage has high-illustration-dependent text containing information-dense illustrations.

A reading passage may have complex illustrations that are accompanied by too few cues. In this case, it might be appropriate to add some instructor-originated questions to direct a student through critical text illustrations. Of course, students may not recognize the functional difference between a chart and a graph. It is important for a teacher to evaluate the visual-literacy base of the students in a class. Students see some illustrations the same way some Americans watch an English cricket game; they know something is going on, but they do not know what it is.

A visually literate classroom instructor should employ his or her talent to evaluate the illustration content of the course textbook. Of course, it would be better to do this at textbook adoption time. Begin by applying Thompson's textbook organization standards to the book and find out how the book is really organized. Choose passages of the book and determine the degree to which the text is illustration dependent. Apply Goldsmith's or Twyman's illustration-type profile to the text illustrations to determine the thrust of their approach. Are the illustrations embedded in the corresponding text, or do they lead or follow text segments? Does the textbook's illustration plan favor high-verbal-ability or low-verbal-ability students? Are there illustrations in the teacher's edition? Is there an identifiable illustration plan for the resource materials? These are some of the questions that a visually literate instructor should raise at textbook adoption time.

One last suggestion: As you teach from a text, form opinions on how well certain sections of the book work. As you discover particularly good or poor sections, note those passages and why they did or did not work for your students. Several teachers have employed a strategy of having their students critique the textbook at the end of each grading period as a device to have the students reconsider what they read that period. Write the publisher or the author, and let them know about your observations. This suggestion is extremely important when considering the illustrations in a textbook. Too often illustrations are overlooked when a book is critiqued. Illustrations have assumed a major role in textbook design so quickly that field feedback is still limited. What little mail publishers receive usually concerns the text prose and not the illustrations. Remember "Beware of pretty pictures . . . for they may lead one astray." Are you visually literate?

References

Alesandrini, K. L., and Rigney, J. W. (1981). Pictorial presentation and review strategies in science learning. *Journal of Research in Science Teaching, 18*(5), 465–474.

Apple, M. W. (1984). The political economy of text publishing. *Educational Theory, 34*(4), 307–319.

Barufaldi, J. P., and Daily, R. J. (1986). Enhancing the reading comprehension of secondary school science textbooks: Suggestions for textbook writers. *Science Education in Ohio, 4*(1), 27–37.

Bernhardt, E. B. (1987). The text as a participant in instruction. *Theory into Practice, 26*(1), 32–37.

Berry, K., and Lee, D. (1982). Readability and the choice of textbooks. *Journal of College Science Teaching, 11*(3), 152–157.

Bertin, J. (1980). The basic test of the graph: A matrix theory of graph construction and cartography. In P. A. Kolers, M. E. Wrolstad, and H. Bouma (Eds.), *Processing of visible language 2* (pp. 585–604). Plenum Press: New York.

Blystone, R. V. (1987a). Post-secondary level knowledge of plant cell fine structure. *Journal of College Science Teaching, 15*(5), 437–443.

Blystone, R. V. (1987b). College introductory biology textbooks. *American Biology Teacher, 49*(7), 418–425.

Blystone, R. V., and Barnard, K. (1988). The future direction of college biology textbooks. *BioScience, 28*(1), 48–52.

Bowler, M. (1978). The making of a textbook. *Learning, 6*(7), 38–42.

Champagne, A. (1987). Middle school science texts: What is wrong that could be made right. *Science Books and Films, 22*(5), 273–281.

Dale, E., and Chall, J. S. (1958). A formula for predicting readability. In C. W. Hunnicutt and W. J. Iverson (Eds.), *Research into the 3R's*. Harper: New York.

Davies, M. J. (1986). Making kids read junk. *Curriculum Review, 26*(2), 11.

DeSilva, B. (1986). Better textbooks? Dim outlook ahead. *Curriculum Review, 26*(2), 8–11.

Doblin, J. (1980). A structure of nontextual communications. In P. A. Kolers, M. E. Wrolstad, and H. Bouma (Eds.), *Processing of visible Language 2* (pp. 89–111). Plenum Press: New York.

Duchastel, P. C. (1978). Illustrating instructional texts. *Educational Technology, 18*(11), 36–39.

Duchastel, P. C., and Waller, R. (1979). Pictorial illustration in instructional texts. *Educational Technology, 19*(11), 20–25.

Duchastel, P. C. (1980). Textbook illustration: Research and instructional design. In: *Educational media yearbook 1980* (pp. 58–63). Edited by J. W. Brown Libraries Unlimited: Littleton, CO.

Duchastel, P. C. (1983). Text illustration is an art—There is no doubt about it. *Performance and Instruction Journal, 22*(3), 3–5.

Dwyer, F. M. (1972). The effects of overt responses in improving visually programmed science instruction. *Journal of Research in Science Teaching, 9*(1), 47–55.

Evans, M. A., Watson, C., and Willows, D. M. (1987). A naturalistic inquiry into illustrations in instructional textbooks. In D. A. Houghton and E. M. Willows (Eds.), *The psychology of illustration volume 2—Instructional issues* (pp. 86–115). Springer-Verlag: New York.

Fiske, E. B. (1984). Are they "dumbing down" the textbooks? *Principal, 64*(2), 44–46.

Fleming, M. L. (1987). Designing pictorial/verbal instruction: Some speculative extensions from research to practice. In D. A. Houghton and E. M. Willows (Eds.), *The psychology of illustration volume 2—Instructional issues* (pp. 136–157). Springer-Verlag: New York.

Flesch, R. F. (1948). A new readability yardstick. *Journal of Applied Psychology, 32*(3), 221–233.

Foster, J. J. (1979). The use of visual cues in text. In P. A. Kolers, M. E. Wrolstad, and H. Bouma (Eds.), *Processing of visible language 1* (pp. 189–203). Plenum Press: New York.

Fry, E. (1977). Fry's readability graph: Clarifications, validity, and extension to level 17. *Journal of Reading, 21*(3), 242–252.

Gabel, D. L. (1983). What high school chemistry texts do well and what they do poorly. *Journal of Chemical Education, 60*(10), 893–895.

Goldsmith, E. (1984). *Research into illustration: An approach and a review* (487 pp). Cambridge University Press: Cambridge.

Goldsmith, E. (1987). The analysis of illustration in theory and practice. In D. A. Houghton and E. M. Willows (Eds.), *The psychology of illustration volume 2—Instructional issues* (pp. 53–85). Springer-Verlag: New York.

Goldstein, P. (1978). *Changing the American school book.* Heath: Lexington, MA. 149 pp.

Gwyn, C. (1987). The well-read textbook. *The Science Teacher, 54*(3), 38–40.

Hayes, D. A., and Readence, J. E. (1983). Transfer of learning from illustration-dependent text. *Journal of Educational Research, 76*(4), 245–248.

Herron, J. D. (1983). What research says and how it can be used. *Journal of Chemical Education, 60*(10), 888–890.

Holliday, W. G. (1975). The effects of verbal and adjunct pictorial-verbal information in science instruction. *Journal of Research in Science Teaching, 12*(1), 77–83.

Holliday, W. G. (1981). Selective attentional effects of textbook study questions on student learning in science. *Journal of Research in Science Teaching, 18*(4), 283–289.

Holliday, W. G., Brunner, L. L., and Donais, E. L. (1977). Differential cognitive and affective response to flow diagrams in science. *Journal of Research in Science Teaching, 14*(2), 129–138.

Holliday, W. G., and Harvey, D. A. (1976). Adjunct labeled drawings in teaching physics to junior high school students. *Journal of Research in Science Teaching, 13*(1), 37–43.

Kauchak, D., Eggen, P., and Kirk, S. (1978). The effect of cue specificity on learning from graphic materials in science. *Journal of Research in Science Teaching, 15*(6), 499–503.

Levie, W. H. (1987). Research on pictures: A guide to the literature. In D. A. Houghton and E. M. Willows (Eds.), *The psychology of illustration volume 1—Basic research* (pp. 1–50). Springer-Verlag: New York.

Levin, R. J., Anglin, G. J., and Carney, R. N. (1987). On empirically validating functions of pictures in prose. In D. A. Houghton and E. M. Willows (Eds.), *The psychology of illustration volume 1—Basic research* (pp. 51–85). Springer-Verlag: New York.

Lynch, P. P., and Strube, P. D. (1985). Ten decades of the science textbook: A revealing mirror of science education past and present. *Journal of Science and Mathematics Education in Southeast Asia, 8*(2), 31–42.

McInerney, J. D. (1986). Biology textbooks—Whose business? *The American Biology Teacher, 48*(7), 396–400.

Mulcahy, P., and Samuels, S. J. (1987). Three hundred years of illustrations in American textbooks. In D. A. Houghton and E. M. Willows (Eds.), *The psychology of illustration volume 2—Instructional issues* (pp. 1–52). Springer-Verlag: New York.

O'Donnell, H. (1985). ERIC/RCS: Improving textbooks—Who is responsible? *Journal of Reading, 29*(3), 268–270.

Osborn, J. H., Jones, B. F., and Stein, M. (1985). The case for improving textbooks. *Educational Leadership, 42*(7), 9–16.

Paine, H. E. (1980). Some problems of illustration. In P. A. Kolers, M. E. Wrolstad, and H. Bouma (Eds.), *Processing of visible language 2* (pp. 143–156). Plenum Press: New York.

Peeck, J. (1987). The role of illustrations in process and remembering illustrated text. In D. A. Houghton and E. M. Willows (Eds.), *The psychology of illustration volume 1—Basic research* (pp. 115–151). Springer-Verlag: New York.

Redei, G. P. (1984). What to look for in selecting college textbooks. *Journal of College Science Teaching, 14*(2), 103–105.

Roller, B. V. (1980). Graph reading abilities of thirteen-year-olds. In P. A. Kolers, M. E. Wrolstad, and H. Bouma (Eds.), *Processing of visible language 2* (pp. 305–314). Plenum Press: New York.

Royer, J. M., and Cable, G. W. (1976). Illustrations, analogies, and facilitative transfer in prose learning. *Journal of Educational Psychology, 68*(2), 205–209.

Schumacher, G. M., and Waller, R. (1985). Testing design alternatives: A comparison of procedures. In T. M. Duffy and R. Waller (Eds.), *Designing usable texts* (pp. 377–403). Academic Press: New York.

Scruggs, T. E., and Mastropieri, M. A. (1985). Illustrative aids improve reading. *Reading Horizons, 25*(2), 108–110.

Smith, B. D., and Elifson, J. M. (1986). Do pictures make a difference in college textbooks? *Reading Horizons, 26*(4), 270–277.

Spiegel, D. L., and Wright, J. D. (1984). Biology teachers' preferences in textbook characteristics. *Journal of Reading, 27*(7), 624–628.

Szlichcinski, K. P. (1980). The syntax of pictorial instructions. In P. A. Kolers, M. E. Wrolstad, and H. Bouma (Eds.), *Processing of visible language 2* (pp. 113–124). Plenum Press: New York.

Talmage, H. (1986). Creating instructional materials: The textbook publisher as connecting link. *Curriculum Review, 26*(1), 8–10.

Thomas, J. L. (1978). The influence of pictorial illustrations with written text and previous achievement on the reading comprehension of fourth grade science students. *Journal of Research in Science Teaching, 15*(5), 401–405.

Thompson, P. J. (1984). *The gatekeepers: Monitors of textbook innovation.* ERIC document 246 402. Paper presented at the 68th annual meeting of the American Educational Research Association.

Twyman, M. (1979). A schema for the study of graphic language (tutorial paper). In P. A. Kolers, M. E., Wrolstad, and H. Bouma (Eds.), *Processing of visible language 1* (pp. 117–150). Plenum Press: New York.

Twyman, M. (1985). Using pictorial language: A discussion of the dimensions of the problem. In T. M. Duffy and R. Waller (Eds.), *Designing usable texts* (pp. 245–312). Academic Press: New York.

Tyson-Berstein, H. (1987). Textbook adoption: The enemy is us. *Curriculum Review 26*(4), 9–11.

Walker, N. (1980). Readability of college general biology textbooks: Revisited. *Science Education, 64*(1), 29–34.

Wandersee, J. H. (1988). Ways students read texts. *Journal of Research in Science Teaching, 25*(1), 69–84.

Winn, W. D. (1987). Charts, graphs, and diagrams in educational materials. In D. A. Houghton and E. M. Willows (Eds.), *The psychology of illustration volume 1—Basic research* (pp. 152–198). Springer-Verlag: New York.

References for Illustrations

Figure 1

BSCS (1980). *Biological science : An inquiry into life*, 4th edition (p. 90). Harcourt, Brace, Jovanovich: New York, NY.

Figure 2a

Oram, R. F. (1983). *Biology: Living systems*, 4th edition (p. 75). Charles E. Merrill: Columbus, OH.

Figure 2b

Goodman, H. D., Emmel, T. C., Graham, L. E., Slowiczek, F. M., and Schechter, Y. (1986.) *Biology* (p. 102.) Harcourt, Brace, Jovanovich: Orlando, FL.

Figure 2c

Towle, A. (1989). *Modern biology* (p. 67). Holt Rinehart & Winston: Austin, TX.

Figure 2d

BSCS (1985). *Biological science : A molecular approach* (p. 128). D. C. Heath: Lexington, MA.

Figure 2e

McLaren, J. E., and Rotundo, L. (1985). *Heath biology* (p. 71). D. C. Heath: Lexington, MA.

Figure 3

Becker, W. (1986). *The world of cells* (p. 329). Benjamin/Cummings: Palo Alto, CA.

Implications of Teachers' Conceptions of Science Teaching and Learning

Edward L. Smith

Michigan State University
East Lansing, Michigan

The focus of this volume is the implications of recent developments in cognition for science education. Most of the chapters deal with aspects of student cognition. This chapter, however, deals primarily with teacher cognition. The cognitive revolution in psychology has contributed new insights into the nature of teacher thinking as well as student thinking. These developments provide the basis for a new understanding of teachers' professional knowledge, what teachers know and the consequences of differences in teachers' knowledge, and what teachers need to know to teach effectively. Thus, these developments have important implications for the improvement of preservice and inservice teacher education and for meeting the needs of teachers for relevant information on how to improve their teaching.

The story begins with a description of some teachers' explanations of a common classroom phenomenon: the failure of some of their students to understand the main ideas of a unit they had been studying. The explanations come from a study of 13 middle-school science teachers as they taught the topics of photosynthesis, cellular respiration, and ecological matter cycling. In addition to administering pre- and post-tests to the students and observing lessons from the teachers' units, we interviewed each teacher, asking them to reflect on their teaching and their students' response to it.

Our post-test results indicated that the proportion of students understanding the main ideas varied considerably across teachers and topics. So did the teachers' explanations of why some of their students failed to understand these ideas. The following are representative explanations offered by the teachers (Hollon and Anderson, 1987):

> "They can't read . . . they can't write . . . and they probably didn't want to try very hard anyway."

> "They can't do anything abstract at all."

> "It's just the ability of the kids through the whole thing. They either have the ability to understand this type of reasoning or they don't. It's like there are smart ones and not-so-smart ones."

> "If they didn't get it the first two times, they're not going to get it no matter what, so there's no sense keeping after them about it."

"They didn't remember what we said about plants using oxygen as well as carbon dioxide."

"It's really difficult for these kids to follow these ideas because they involve a lot of steps."

"They still think that plants only do photosynthesis and people have respiration."

"They still haven't gotten away from the idea that respiration is just breathing . . . after awhile some, maybe most, will get to the point where they can explain more about the cell part."

"They get confused . . . and so they go back to what they know best . . . they haven't worked it through yet."

"They just repeat what's in the question . . . it takes a long time to get them over the non-answer stuff."

The results of this and other studies indicate that these different explanations reflect more than differences among the students. They also reflect differences in the teachers' conceptions. For example, some of the above explanations focus on basic skills or motivation, while others focus on the nature of their content-specific knowledge. These different conceptions tend to lead to different decisions and actions, and ultimately, to different student learning results. An explanation in terms of the students' lack of basic skills would imply that teachers should lower their expectations for student accomplishment and/or students should receive remedial teaching. Explanations emphasizing a lack of motivation might imply that teachers ought to do fun activities or, if this condition is viewed as beyond the control of the teacher, lower expectations for student achievement. Explanations emphasizing the complexity of tasks or content might imply the need to lower expectations by assigning simpler tasks and content. Explanations in terms of students' failure to remember might imply a need for more review and repetition of content. Explanations in terms of the persistence of students' old ways of thinking could imply that teachers should identify students' misconceptions and address them directly in instruction to help students change them.

In explaining student failure to learn, many teachers referred to factors that are difficult for teachers to influence, such as the students' ability levels or the nature of the subject matter. Some teachers, however, emphasized factors that can be addressed more directly. We will explore one explanation of particular importance in its implications for teaching and learning, which refers to specific ways in which students' existing ideas differ from those being promoted through instruction. A growing body of research indicates that many students' problems in understanding scientific ideas result from such differences.

Students do not come to the study of a science topic as blank slates (if they did they would be unable to understand at all). Rather, they bring with them relevant conceptions through which they attempt to make sense of what they hear, read, and observe. These conceptions are primarily products of the students' experience with the everyday world and, in fact, fit that world quite adequately for many purposes. However, these homegrown conceptions (which I will hereafter refer to as "naive") are often inconsistent with or even contradict the scientific conceptions which underlie the science content to which the students are exposed. Therefore, students' efforts to understand this content often result in misinterpretations through selective attention and interpretation of information in terms of their naive conceptions.

Even more commonly, students give up the attempt to understand science content. The new information often seems counterintuitive and just does not fit their ways of thinking. As a result, students conclude that science does not make sense and resort to memorization or other non-sensemaking strategies to cope with the demands of science instruction (Roth, in press). Although this approach often results in satisfactory grades, it is also probably the basis for decisions to escape science at the first opportunity.

While these differences between students' everyday conceptions and more scientific alternatives represent what D. Hawkins (1980) calls "critical barriers" to learning in science, they also represent important keys to student understanding. A number of studies have found that when instruction specifically addresses such differences, substantial increases in the proportion of students who understand the scientific ideas can be achieved. Such results, however, are not obtained simply by telling students that their ideas are wrong and the alternative is right. Rather, students need to be convinced. For students to change their ways of thinking about natural phenomena, they must begin to develop dissatisfaction with their old ways of thinking, develop an initial grasp of the new scientific alternative, and gradually develop commitment to it as they find it fruitful in a variety of applications (Posner, Strike, Hewson, and Gertzog, 1982). Instruction is not likely to establish these conditions unless teachers confront students' naive conceptions and teach for conceptual change.

An Example of Conceptual-Change Teaching

This illustration of conceptual-change teaching is based on a study conducted by J. Minstrell (1984), a high-school physics teacher, supported by a grant from the National Science Foundation (NSF) for a project in which student learning was examined over a two-year period. The study focused on the topic of force and motion.

In the year prior to Minstrell's study, results from his unit test indicated that only about 30 percent of his students understood and consistently applied the Newtonian conception of force and motion. Rather than attributing this failure to a lack of basic skills or low motivation on the part of the students, or to the abstractness of the concepts, Minstrell attributed a major part of the problem to the persistence of naive conceptions to which the students were committed when they entered the course. His results and others (Clement, 1982; Viennot, 1983) revealed that many students believe that any motion of an object requires the action of force on that object. (In contrast, the Newtonian view is that objects in motion remain in motion unless acted upon by a force.) In the absence of any external force on a moving object, students posit various "forces" from previous events that are "used up" as the object moves. Such "forces" are not necessary (and do not exist) in a Newtonian view.

Many students retain their non-Newtonian views even after studying physics at high-school and college levels (Champagne, Gunstone, and Klopfer, 1983; and Clement, 1982). Without a change in students' conceptions, statements of Newton's laws remained empty verbalisms, and formulas such as $F = ma$ were only learned by rote and mechanically applied. By approaching the subject under these circumstances, many students received the implicit message that science just doesn't make sense and that they are not very good in it.

Over a two-year period, Minstrell devised and revised instructional strategies aimed at helping students make this basic conceptual change concerning force and objects. According to Minstrell:

> I was convinced I could do better. During the first year of systematic investigation I carefully redesigned the instruction to make the students aware of their initial conceptions about forces on moving objects, to have them experience some typical

sorts of laboratory activities (that relate to Newton's Laws), and to use rational argument to show what forces are necessary to explain the motions. Throughout the unit, foremost in my mind was an awareness of the difficulties students have with Newton's Laws, particularly the First Law, and whenever opportunity existed, I recycled rational arguments in favor of Newton's Laws. With this instruction reflecting a keen awareness of difficulties students have in understanding Newton's Laws, the percentage of the class displaying a Newtonian view on the semester test (three months after the unit) was 71 percent in the acceleration cases and 67 percent in the constant velocity cases. (pp. 59–60)

In the second year, Minstrell was hoping for even higher percentages. Noting that a consistently higher proportion of students gave Newtonian explanations for the accelerating cases than for the constant velocity cases, he wondered why. He also noted that "the concrete firsthand experience in the instruction dealt with situations involving acceleration, Newton's Second Law." Invoking the Piagetian principle of moving from the concrete to the abstract, he reversed the traditional order of instruction and began with investigation of accelerated motion. A critical observation was the uniform acceleration that results when a constant force (as indicated on a spring scale) was applied to a low-friction cart. It became a point of leverage in subsequent discussions of both accelerated and constant velocity cases.

With this further change in instruction, the percentage of students demonstrating Newtonian reasoning for *both* accelerated and constant velocity cases on the semester test was about 80 percent, indicating that an additional 10 percent of the students had made this important conceptual change.

Thus, while some students might lack important basic skills, or might be unwilling to make an effort to learn, Minstrell's study and others like it indicate that instruction that considers the nature of students' incoming knowledge and patterns of thinking can be much more effective in helping a majority of the students understand the subject matter.

Why Isn't This Kind of Teaching More Common?

In the previous section, I argued that teaching which addresses students' naive conceptions enables a substantially greater proportion of students to understand scientific conceptions than instruction that does not. In light of this argument, the question arises, Why isn't this kind of teaching more common? My answer in brief is that many teachers lack the knowledge they would need to teach this way.

Let's consider the case of Minstrell's improved success with the topic of force and motion. As he began his study, Minstrell already had a solid understanding of Newtonian mechanics and could apply it to explain everyday phenomena and laboratory experiments. However, he also knew from recent research that his students, like many others, held an alternative view. Thus, he came to view his task as somehow getting his students to change their minds.

Minstrell developed or selected laboratory activities and constructed questions that would frame the key issues, bring out students' naive conceptions, and challenge them. He developed a strategy of engaging the students in debates using data and arguments. Over the period of the study, he learned more about the students' naive conceptions and how they influenced the students' interpretations of the experiments and their answers to the questions. On this basis, he revised his approach with the result that he was able to help most of his students make the intended changes in their thinking.

Thus, over the course of the study, Minstrell had come to possess important new knowledge, including knowledge of

• his students' naive conceptions

• ways these conceptions contrasted with the scientific conception he wanted them to develop

• activities and his students' thinking about them

• teaching strategies that would help students come to change their way of thinking about the topic

Furthermore, Minstrell was able to share this knowledge with a colleague to the extent that she too made a substantial improvement in the proportion of students adopting a Newtonian view of force and motion.

Results of a number of other studies, including several by my colleagues and me at Michigan State University, also indicate that when teachers have the topic-specific knowledge needed to understand students' naive conceptions and combat them, teachers can be substantially more effective in helping their students discard some conceptions, modify others, and finally come to understand the scientific topic being studied (Anderson and Smith, 1987).

Researchers have now examined students' naive conceptions for a substantial number of topics and have developed a modest base of knowledge about activities and teaching strategies effective in promoting these conceptual changes. However, teacher education and curriculum development are just beginning to reflect these developments.

Why haven't more teachers developed such knowledge on their own? From my own research experience, I can testify that this is by no means a simple task. It took Minstrell two years of effort on a single topic, and few teachers have the time and resources that Minstrell or research programs such as ours at Michigan State have been able to devote.

Aside from the lack of time and resources, however, there is a more basic reason. Just as researchers' theories have led them in other directions until recently, so most teachers' conceptions of learning and their role in promoting it led them in other directions. Recall the teachers' explanations of students' failure to understand from the beginning of the article. These explanations reflect alternative conceptions held by teachers. What are these conceptions and what difference do they make?

Teachers' Conceptions of Science Teaching and Learning

The studies that my colleagues and I have carried out over the last ten years have involved not only extensive classroom observation, testing, and interviewing of students; we have also observed, conducted interviews, and had extensive informal interactions with teachers. One of the major outcomes of this research has been the identification of differing conceptions that *teachers* hold of science teaching and learning, and an understanding of some of their consequences. We have found that these conceptions influence not only teachers' approaches to teaching, but also the kinds of information they find relevant and therefore tend to seek and value. Thus, these conceptions have consequences in the course of the development of teachers' professional knowledge. These conceptions are defined as follows in terms of the teachers' views of

• what students should be learning

• how learning occurs

• the teachers' roles in promoting learning

Fact Acquisition. As implied by the label, this conception is characterized by a view of the subject matter of science as consisting of a series of facts and definitions to be learned. This conception is reflected in the following comment by "Mr. Armstrong" (a pseudonym) referring to the specially designed text we had provided as part of the middle-school science study briefly described in the introduction:

You could take every other paragraph or two paragraphs and end up with what you could teach the kids or maybe one sentence of it that was important, so why deal with the rest? . . .

For this age group, you have to eliminate as much of the garbage as you can and get down to nothing but the facts. You aren't going to keep their attention long enough to do much else . . . you are just going to confuse the kids. (Hollon and Anderson, 1987, p. 33)

The superfluous material or "garbage" to which the teacher referred was information that related one idea to another, challenged common naive conceptions, or gave real-world applications. The fact-acquisition conception represents the structure of the subject matter as list-like, a sequence of more or less independent facts rather than a network of interconnected ideas. The learning of these facts seems to be an end in itself, or the way to pass tests and courses, rather than a means of enabling explanation, prediction, description, and control of phenomena.

The role of the teacher in this conception is to expose students to the facts to be learned and provide activities that require students to locate, recognize, or recall them. Teachers' concerns tend to focus less on learning per se than on students' task completion and maintenance of interest and involvement. Thus, audio-visual aids are often preferred for their attention-holding value. Implicit in this conception is a view of learning as receiving and remembering information, in which individual facts are stored in memory more or less as received, to be recalled when needed. With this view of teaching and learning, failure to succeed is logically viewed as resulting from a lack of effort or basic skills.

This pattern of thinking about teaching and learning is probably most common among teachers with relatively weak science backgrounds. Teachers with stronger science backgrounds, however, may also have this conception when they perceive rote memorization as the only kind of learning of which their students are capable, or as the only kind that the predominant testing regime will tolerate.

Content Understanding. The fundamental contrast between the content-understanding and fact-acquisition conceptions lies in what the students are to learn. Teachers with the content-understanding conception typically have a mature understanding of the content and intend that their students come to share it. The structure of subject matter is understood as interconnected ideas which are exemplified by and help explain natural phenomena. Teachers with the content-understanding conception believe their role is to present this content in a logical way to reflect its structure and organization, and to do so in a way that is both interesting and intelligible to the students. They value demonstrations and laboratory experiences which develop the story line. These teachers are less concerned with task completion for its own sake and more concerned with whether or not the students have understood the subject matter.

While teachers with the content-understanding conception contrast sharply with teachers having the fact-acquisition conception in their views of what is to be learned, their views of learning itself are not that different. In both conceptions, learning is primarily a matter of receiving and storing information. The assumption of the content-understanding conception is that students will add the new information to previously presented information in the appropriate way. A clear presentation and sufficient student study of information should result in the students having it appropriately organized and stored in memory. Teachers believe that the presented information carries much the same meaning for the student as it does for the presenter.

When students fail to understand or remember, it is interpreted as resulting from unclear presentation, lack of effort on the part of the students, or lack of sufficient aptitude for learning the kind of content being taught. Because teachers can only directly control presentation, their efforts to improve focus primarily on revisions in lectures, textbooks, and, perhaps, laboratory examples to better develop the story line.

This conception is probably most common at the college and high-school levels but is also found at the middle-school level. "Mr. Barnes" was one of the teachers in our middle-school science study. His science background was probably the strongest of any of the teachers in the study. In his teaching, he made explicit connections among ideas, related ideas from labs to lectures, and included examples from the history of science illustrating aspects of the nature of science. In spite of all of his efforts to help students understand the subject matter, however, he did not expect to achieve this goal, "except maybe for that 20 percent in the class you observed. . . ." For the others,

> I think we are kind of giving them a little bit of information and help them toss some ideas around and when they get into high school they are going to go into these things a little more deeply. If they are really serious about it, if these things are important to a few of them, they go from there and really begin to learn and understand it, but not the majority. (Roth, 1987, p. 35)

Mr. Barnes was characterized by K. J. Roth (1987) as developing "very content dense, lecture dominated lessons." He added considerable detail to our conceptual-change oriented materials which he considered to be "very watered down." As Roth explained,

> On the first two days of the photosynthesis unit, for example, he explained all of the following ideas, none of which was mentioned in the photosynthesis materials: molecular structure of chlorophyll, compounds, carbon atoms, atomic arrangement of carbon dioxide and water molecules, sucrose, transpiration, palisade cells, spongy cells, chloroplasts, auxins, hormones, tropisms, positive phototropism, hardening, adaptations, temperate zone, atomic energy, stomata, fats, oils, starches, fibers, proteins, carbohydrates. (pp. 37–38)

Mr. Barnes' view of learning as primarily taking in and organizing information is implicit in his teaching strategies and is also reflected in comments in which he refers to "giving" students "information," or "programming the information into them."

Mr. Barnes was aware of the limited number of students who understood and even of some of the misconceptions that students held. However, he viewed these simply as indicators of a lack of understanding rather than as keys to achieving understanding.

> After five years on something—I can predict what they are going to get stuck on. And so I'll kind of plan it in spaces to cover that particular thing again, because I know they are going to get hung up on a certain thing. (pp. 33–34)

Mr. Barnes, with his knowledge of student misconceptions, could have debated his students and changed their minds—instead these were things for *him* to "cover" again.

Conceptual Change. This conception was implicit in Minstrell's case studies described above. Although this conception leads to differences in content emphasis from the two prior conceptions, the view of the subject matter to be learned is similar to that of the content-understanding perspective. Both view the subject matter as interconnected ideas related to phenomena. The fundamental contrast between these two conceptions lies in teachers' beliefs about the nature of learning and how these play out in their decisions. In the conceptual-change conception, teachers view students as *constructing* their ideas about the world rather than simply receiving them. "Ms. Copeland," another teacher in our study, put it this way:

> Teachers who lecture then leave them spit it back at you . . . they see themselves as dispensers of information . . . their whole expectation of "I know" is a lot different. If the kid can spit it back at you on the test Monday, then he knows it— No! I don't think he knows it at all. (Hollon and Anderson, 1987, p. 14)

Students selectively attend to and interpret what they hear, read, and observe. Thus the knowledge that students construct is only partially influenced by the new information that the teacher presents. Instead their understanding is also heavily influenced by the ideas and patterns of thinking they already have, much of which consists of naive conceptions based on personal experience with everyday phenomena and language.

Teachers with the conceptual-change conception believe that the information they present to classes is not generally a very good representation of what the students are likely to construct. Thus, the unique role for the teacher with this perspective is to monitor students' current ideas and ways of thinking and to plan subsequent instruction to guide the students in constructing more adequate knowledge. Minstrell's improved success resulted from his awareness of his students' naive conception that motion of an object implied a force acting on it, his planning and use of activities to challenge this view, and his continuous monitoring of the effects of instruction on his students' thinking.

Teachers like Minstrell view the students' knowledge as the ideas to which the students are committed, not just the information that students can produce on command. Thus, such teachers use evidence and debate in the context of applications so that students become convinced of the greater power and "fruitfulness" of the new idea.

While the content-understanding teacher focuses primarily on the structure and organization of the subject matter presented, the conceptual-change teacher's primary focus of attention is the current state of the student's ideas and its relationship to the standard story. It is this difference in focus that leads to differences in emphasis in subject matter between the two conceptions. Whereas the content-understanding teacher bases content-selection decisions primarily on the structure of the subject matter, the conceptual-change teacher generally makes content decisions that are strategically useful in helping students develop a particular idea, but whose rationale is not evident from considerations of the structure of the subject matter alone. This rationale emerges from consideration of both the structure of the subject matter and the students' current ideas as well as the similarities and contrasts between them.

Curricular debates on the issue of breadth versus depth in subject-matter selection may be based on differences in thinking about science learning and teaching. Whereas educators with the content-understanding conception tend to view depth of knowledge in terms of sophistication of theory and elaboration of detail, the conceptual-change conception educators view depth in terms of the degree to which students incorporate and apply basic ideas in their own ways of thinking about phenomena in the everyday world (Anderson, 1989).

Consequences of Alternative Conceptions of Science Teaching and Learning for Teachers' Professional Development

The alternative conceptions of teaching and learning just described are summarized and contrasted in Table 1 in terms of their views of what is learned, how learning occurs, and the teacher's role in promoting learning. These conceptions have important consequences in the immediate effects that they have on teaching and learning. However, even more important are the long-range consequences. Teachers' conceptions of teaching and learning influence their development of professional knowledge over time and their response to new information which they encounter. One might expect that these alternative conceptions reflect levels of professional development with the fact-acquisition conception developing into the content-understanding conception, and that in turn to the conceptual-change conception. However,

TABLE 1			
Alternative Conceptions of Science Teaching and Learning			
Conception	**Issue**		
	What is to be learned	*How learning occurs*	*Teacher roles*
Fact Acquisition	List of the facts and definitions	By receiving and remembering the information presented; repetition	Expose students to the facts, drill; motivate students by finding interesting media to use
Content Understanding	Important ideas in the discipline	By receiving and comprehending content, looking for relationships, trying to understand	Present and explain content in a coherent and interesting way, using examples, demonstrations, and labs to illustrate
Conceptual Development	Important ideas in the discipline and their application to the real world	By interpreting/ constucting representations of what is read, heard, and observed; integrating with and changing prior ideas to make sense	Monitor students' ideas and interpretations; present alternatives; lead students into dissatisfaction with old ideas toward alternative ideas through application, evidence, and argument

this may not be the case. Our results suggest that each conception is self-reinforcing, leading to a form of development within its own framework but not necessarily pointing toward the other conceptions (Hollon and Anderson, 1987).

Teachers' conceptions of science learning and teaching influence what they attend to in curriculum materials, the kinds of information they seek, and their perceptions of what they need in order to do a better job. In our study of middle-school science teaching, this pattern is reflected in teachers' attention to and use of information in our curriculum materials.

Mr. Armstrong, representing a fact-acquisition conception, did not seem to value the information about students' naive conceptions or the rationale for the conceptual-change activities and teaching strategies. In his words,

I did skim it (the respiration teachers' guide) a bit. What I found was my conceptions on it and that my feelings were on it were about the same as the book, so it wasn't worth my time to go through each area . . . there wasn't that much variance. . . .

I just felt that I didn't need it. I just kind of felt out what the kids were dealing with . . . it wasn't that important to me because I didn't spend that much time with them on it. I kind of let them dig into it and get the information out of it (the student text). (Hollon and Anderson, 1987, p. 34)

Mr. Armstrong, like the other fact-acquisition teachers in our study, showed little awareness of the students' naive conceptions. More important, however, he did not see any reason to learn about them. In his view, as a teacher you find materials that "get down to nothing but the facts" and then let the students "dig into it and get the information out." This was how he interpreted and used our curriculum materials.

Mr. Barnes, reflecting a content-understanding conception, reported that he used our student texts in planning to get "some sense of the direction the students should be headed," but referred to his college texts to "refresh my memory and think about important ideas" (Hollon and Anderson, 1987, pp. 23–24). His teaching reflected a deep and interconnected understanding of the subject matter.

Concerning our information about students' naive conceptions, Mr. Barnes said, "I kind of know the kinds of mistakes the students are going to make," and unlike Mr. Armstrong he was quite accurate in predicting students' responses to diagnostic questions. Given Mr. Barnes' knowledge of the subject matter and his awareness of the students' difficulty and naive conceptions, he probably stood to gain the most from learning about the conceptual-change strategies modeled in our curriculum materials. However, his interpretations or adaptive modifications of the approach resulted in what Roth termed "empty use" of the strategies. Our focus on a small number of important issues that are problematic for students was interpreted as "watering down" the curriculum. The introduction of a large amount of additional content information blurred that focus. Whereas our materials suggested beginning with a series of questions to elicit the children's ideas, Mr. Barnes began with a detailed explanation of photosynthesis. When he did pose the questions on the second day of instruction, none of the responses reflected understanding of the previously presented content. Nonetheless, he continued his teaching-by-telling approach with minilectures, addressing the students' naive conceptions one-by-one rather than engaging the students in constructing and puzzling through these issues themselves.

A similar pattern emerged in Mr. Barnes' use of application questions. Instead of allowing students to struggle through construction of explanations, he often simply presented the correct answers himself. When students were allowed to answer, he quickly identified or gave the correct answer and elaborated on it himself rather than probing student responses and helping them reason through the problems. This pattern represents empty use of the suggested teaching strategies.

Thus, both Mr. Armstrong's and Mr. Barnes' conception of science learning and teaching influenced their perception of what information was necessary and valuable to them as teachers. They seemed to have self-reinforcing belief systems which limited their access to new information that might have made them more effective in helping students understand science. Ms. Copeland, reflecting a conceptual-change conception, demonstrated quite a different response to the information in our materials. Commenting on our charts contrasting scientific and naive conceptions in the photosynthesis teacher's guide, she said:

I can gain a lot from seeing those and thinking, OK here are some things that I can anticipate and head off. . . .

So that in my discussion of them I can say, "So does that mean . . . whatever the naive conception is?" And they'll say, "no, no . . . " and I know they've got it and if they say, "yeah . . . right," then I know we've got a problem. (Hollon and Anderson, 1987, p. 13)

Expressing her appreciation of the application activities, she commented:

They make the kids apply what they have learned about and figure things out rather than just copy stuff down from the book. . . .

They had to work things through and use what they know about the functions of those things in order to work them out . . . that's applying all the other stuff. (p. 13)

This is how she used the activities. Here she describes (quite accurately) her use of application questions in the respiration unit:

I kept coming back to those three questions. . . . Why a person dies when their heart stops? . . . Why do we eat? . . . Why do we breathe? . . . especially the first one because they would say "so what?" And I kept after them until they could tell me "so what?" And they really had to know the information in these other things to be able to tell me and keep me from badgering them about why. But if I had not asked them that question, I think they would have just memorized . . . they would have been able to identify the right words in the right places on the test and not have understood a thing . . . not understood what this had to do with them or living things or life functions at all. (p. 13)

Given the same materials and teaching suggestions, Ms. Copeland found much more of value to her than did either Mr. Armstrong or Mr. Barnes. Furthermore, she used the strategies to develop additional insights into her students' thinking.

These examples illustrate how teachers' conceptions of science learning and teaching influence their interpretation of curriculum materials and their attention to and use of different kinds of information. Extending these patterns over time suggests that these conceptions can lead teachers' professional development in quite different directions.

The *fact-acquisition conception* tends to lead away from subject-matter learning as the central concern. Rather, motivation, management, and a concern with students' task completion become the focus. These teachers want curricula which clearly present the facts to be learned (with little "garbage"), while providing interesting activities and audio-visual materials. This conception, however, does not generally lead to deeper insights into the nature of the subject matter and especially not into insights into students' ways of thinking about science and natural phenomena, even when such information is available.

The *content-understanding conception*, in contrast, generally leads to the improvement of the teacher's knowledge of subject matter and improvements in the organization and richness of the teacher's class presentations and laboratory activities. These teachers tend to improve in their knowledge of what subject matter students can learn more easily and what will take more effort. In particular, the concept-understanding conception is likely to lead to an awareness that many students do not understand the subject matter as well as the teacher had intended.

Further, the teachers discover that continued efforts to improve presentations and laboratory activities, etc., yield dwindling payoffs in improved student learning. When teachers attribute this failure exclusively to factors over which they have little control, factors such as the aptitude or effort of the students and the abstractness of the subject matter, then progress ceases.

Even when content-understanding teachers become aware of some student misconceptions, they view the misconceptions of students more as evidence of lack of understanding rather than as keys to the development of understanding.

The *conceptual-change conception*, reflected in Minstrell's study and Ms. Copeland from our middle-school science study, uniquely emphasizes the value of understanding student conceptions and interpretations. Teachers with this conception believe that most students can understand if the critical barriers in student conceptions can be identified and appropriate evidence or argument found to surmount them. Progress never ceases because this view leads teachers to continued efforts to revise instruction, looking for a new insight into their students' thinking and the specific question, phenomenon, or argument that will convince a few more students to change their minds on a key issue.

Teaching science so that the majority of students understand is possible but requires a considerable amount of topic-specific knowledge of typical student naive conceptions and teaching strategies for promoting the necessary conceptual changes. Teachers without conceptual-change conceptions of teaching and learning seem unlikely to develop and use such knowledge on their own. Fact-acquisition and content-understanding conceptions represent self-reinforcing belief systems which lead teachers in other directions.

Implications

In the first section of this chapter, I argued that developments in science educa-tion and supporting disciplines, including psychology and philosophy of science, offer the possibility of substantial improvement in the understanding of science for a majority of students. Key to this possibility is the development and use of a professional knowledge base for science education, including both the guiding conceptions of learning and teaching and detailed topic-specific knowledge. The guiding conceptions are emerging in science-education literature, and a beginning has been made in the development of a topic-specific knowledge base. However, these developments are only beginning to affect the classroom.

In the second section of the paper, I described commonly held conceptions of teaching and learning, and I discussed their consequences for teachers' development of new professional knowledge.

The developments described have important implications for teachers, policy makers, teacher educators, and curriculum developers and researchers. These include the following:

• **Teachers need to adopt the goal of helping a majority of students to understand science.** Such a goal needs to be addressed by policy makers, curriculum developers, and teacher educators as well as by teachers themselves. In particular, this goal needs to be distinguished from one in which understanding is expected of only an elite minority or from one which accepts task completion or factual recall as a standard of success for science teaching.

• **Teachers need to be provided with access to topic-specific knowledge not now available to them.** Neither teacher education nor the curriculum materials generally available provide teachers with the knowledge necessary to bring about the level of understanding of which most students are capable. Furthermore, it is unrealistic to expect teachers to be able to develop this knowledge individually through their own efforts in the classroom. High priority should be given to the development of curriculum materials reflecting these new perspectives and knowledge. Inservice education programs and innovative ways of sharing topic-specific knowledge, such as systematic computer networking, should be implemented.

- **Many teachers will need professional development opportunities to support changes in their conceptions of science teaching and learning.** Many teachers will need to change their conceptions in order to comprehend, value, and use the specific knowledge becoming available. Teachers must be convinced that changes in their ideas and teaching practices are warranted and worthwhile. Substantial professional development opportunities will be required to help teachers accomplish these changes.

- **Schools must recognize and reward teaching for the goal of student understanding for the majority of students.** Teachers cannot be expected to undertake and sustain efforts to address this new goal unless schools provide them with the kind of support necessary and give them recognition and reward when success is achieved. In many situations, teachers receive little recognition for success in promoting student understanding for the majority. Instead, recognition is gained from a high degree of success with a few top students only, or from higher scores on fact-oriented assessment tests.

An important step toward the goal of achieving understanding for the majority of students would be the development of testing programs that generate data on the proportion of students who understand and can apply scientific conceptions for specific topics in the science curriculum. While the initial results of such programs would probably reveal discouraging levels of student performance, they would nevertheless provide the basis for identifying and recognizing improved success as it is accomplished.

- **We should change our assumptions about what it means for a teacher to be a professional.** The emergence of the professional knowledge base described in this chapter provides an additional basis for the case for teaching as a profession. That is, teachers are professional to the extent that they possess a specialized knowledge that enables them to be more successful than those without it, not just because they have control over decision-making processes.

References

Anderson, C. W. (1989). The role of education in the academic disciplines in teacher preparation. In A. Woolfold (Ed.), *The graduate preparation of teachers: Research perspective.* Englewood Cliffs, NJ: Prentice Hall.

Anderson, C. W., and Smith, E. L. (1987). Teaching Science. In V. Roehler, (Ed.), *The educators handbook: A research perspective.* New York: Longman, Inc.

Champagne, A. B., Gunstone, R. F., and Klopfer, L. E. (1983). *Effecting changes in cognitive structures amongst physics students.* Paper presented at the symposium on Stability and Change in Conceptual Understanding, annual meeting of the American Educational Research Association, Montreal.

Clement, J. (1982). Students' preconceptions in introductory physics. *American Journal of Physics, 50,* 66–71.

Hawkins, D. (1980). *Critical barriers to science learning.* Mountain View Center, University of Colorado at Boulder.

Hollon, R. E., and Anderson, C. W. (1987). *Teachers' beliefs about student learning in science.* Paper presented at the annual meeting of the American Education Research Association, Washington, DC.

Minstrell, J. (1984). Teaching for the development of understanding of ideas. Forces on moving objects. In C. W. Anderson (Ed.), *Perspectives from research and practice.* 1984 Yearbook of the Association for the Education of Teachers in Science.

Posner, G. J., Strike, K. A., Hewson, R. W., and Gertzog, W. A. (1982). Accommodation of a scientific conception: Toward a theory of conceptual change. *Science Education, 66*(2), 211–227.

Roth, K. J. (1987, April). *Helping science teachers change: The critical role of teachers' knowledge about science and science learning.* Paper presented at the annual meeting of the American Educational Research Association, Washington, DC.

Roth, K. J. (in press). The challenge of reading science texts for conceptual change. In A. Alvermann and C. Santa (Eds.), *Science learning: Processes and applications.* Hillsdale, NJ: Lawrence Erlbaum.

Viennot, L. (1983). Natural tendencies in analyzing students' reasoning. In H. Helm and J. D. Novak (Eds.), *Misconceptions in science and mathematics.* Ithaca, NY: Cornell University.

Why Girls Don't Know

Jane Butler Kahle
Miami University
Oxford, Ohio

In a 1987 study, researchers approached the results of the 1976–77 National Assessment of Educational Progress (NAEP) for science from a different angle. Rather than looking at only correct and incorrect answers, M. C. Linn, T. de Benedictis, K. Delucchi, A. Harris, and E. Stage also examined the "I don't know" responses. When they compared boys and girls, they found that much of the achievement differences could be accounted for by differences in answering patterns. Girls, significantly more often than boys, selected the "I don't know" response.

Why do so many girls respond, "I don't know?" Are they less knowledgeable, less informed? Or are they more honest, more modest? If girls are to participate more in the sciences, these questions need to be answered. Recent studies of classroom practices and teacher intervention programs suggest some answers to these problems. In order to understand what teachers can do, I will assess the situation and propose some solutions. I will begin with a review of today's science classrooms, elementary through college, followed by a survey of recent programs and their solutions.

Assessing the Situation

According to E. F. Keller (1986), gender is "what a culture makes of sex. It is the cultural transformation of male and female infants into adult men and women" (p. 122). My analysis of *Why Girls Don't Know* is an interpretation of gender differences; that is, differences in interactions not attributable to biological differences, which begin before school and continue throughout life. For example, even though preschool girls and boys are physically similar, they already have very different experiences. Boys' experiences provide them with backgrounds, interests, and attitudes which are important for later achievement in science (Kahle and Lakes, 1983; Sjoberg, 1986). They handle more tools, throw more balls, construct more Lego bridges, build more block towers, and tinker more with simple mechanical objects. In addition, boys generally receive more subtle rewards for taking risks. Exclamations such as, "What a brave boy!" or "Isn't he strong!" reward a boy for climbing trees or jumping into pools. A girl, on the other hand, is praised for "being a little lady" and "keeping her pretty dress clean." While these differences are subtle, they provide one sex with an appropriate background, as well as the necessary attitudes, for success in science. As S. Johnston (1984) observes:

Boys and girls enter school science classrooms with different past experiences, different interests, different attitudes and different expectations. This indicates that teachers cannot dismiss the problem of girls' under-achieving in science by treating boys and girls identically. . . . [T]he science classroom and curriculum are designed to build on a foundation of interests, experience and attitudes that is present for one sex but not for the other. Treating boys and girls identically in school can serve to accentuate rather than diminish the existing differences. (p. 22)

Unfortunately, evidence suggests that girls do not even receive equal treatment in schools, not to mention the kind of treatment needed to encourage them in the sciences. Nothing in the curriculum acts to counter girls' lack of out-of-school science experiences, and this inexperience continues to be a problem throughout elementary and secondary school and into college.

Elementary School

In assessing elementary classrooms, studies indicate that boys and girls bring different science experiences to school, and once in school they receive very different science educations. Studies in England (Smail, 1984), the United States (Kahle and Lakes, 1983), Norway (Jorde and Lea, 1987), and Australia (Parker and Rennie, 1986) document very different behaviors by boys and girls in the elementary classroom. Fewer girls than boys handle science equipment, perform science experiments, or participate in science-related activities. The different backgrounds that boys and girls bring to elementary school are perpetuated by the schools; for example, I. Mullins and L. Jenkins (1988) report that only 37 percent of girls in the third grade, compared with 51 percent of the boys, have used microscopes. Equal numbers of girls and boys may sit through science lessons, but they participate in them in unequal ways.

As W. Harlen (1985) states:

The opportunity for children to experience science activities exists at the elementary-school level perhaps more readily than at later stages of education. If we wish to increase girls' access to science therefore, science at this early level has a vital part to play. (p. 545)

The elementary school is the critical place for change: change in formal and informal science curricula, change in classroom instruction and interactions, and change in school structure and socialization.

When children first enter school, international projects report that although boys and girls express interest in slightly different types of science, their overall levels of interest are similar.

Furthermore, for both boys and girls, interests are directly related to areas of daily experience. For example, L. H. Parker and L. J. Rennie (1986) report the following:

Where the experience is one which is likely to be universal (e.g.,earthworms, shadows, germs, and water), very little sex-differentiation of interest is shown. In other areas, such as wheels and motors and growing a vegetable or flower garden, where boys' and girls' out-of-school experiences are likely to be quite different, clear sex-stereotyping is revealed. (p. 177)

Sex-related differences in out-of-school experiences may be reinforced within schools if children are allowed to select science topics based on interest. Therefore, the elementary science curriculum is extremely important. It must be motivating, yet include a range of topics; it must include opportunities to handle the tools of science, yet develop a conceptual foundation for later studies.

The student-centered, activity-based curricula of the 1960s and 1970s fulfill the criteria for an ideal curriculum. Ironically, they are little used, and when they are implemented, they are frequently misused. These curricula, SCIS (Science Curriculum Improvement Study), SAPA (Science, a Process Approach), and ESS (Elementary Science Study) have faded from classrooms for three primary reasons: Teachers have not understood the scientific principles the materials promulgated, classrooms have not been organized for small group interaction in science, and schools have not provided the equipment or the scheduling required. However, recent analyses make a strong case for experience-based curricula. For example, a review of 34 evaluative studies indicated that children using the "hands-on" curricula performed better on every measure of achievement than children studying "textbook" science. In fact, one analysis of 13,000 children in 1,000 U.S. classrooms has demonstrated that children instructed using activity-based materials surpass those who received traditional instruction. They score higher on tests of science processes, creativity, perception, logic, development, science content, and mathematics. In addition, the experience-based curricula provide opportunities for experimentation as well as for handling instruments, making measurements, observing natural phenomena, collecting data, and making interpretations. These curricula also have the potential of producing equal outcomes for both sexes. As C. Iliams (1985) states, "girls are less likely than boys to make up the education deficiency in out-of-school experiences" (p. 79), therefore a "hands-on" curriculum is necessary in order to provide opportunities for the experimental background which girls lack when they enter school.

Although activity-based curricula may provide needed experiences, teachers must implement them carefully to insure equal opportunity for participation and equal expectation of performance by both sexes. Teachers may need to reorganize classroom activities to provide girls with the extra time and opportunities to do science in order to get the same level of performance that teachers anticipate and encourage from boys. Another obstacle to equal education opportunity is that girls frequently choose not to participate in science demonstrations and experiments in spite of encouragement from teachers. Because socialization discourages girls from science, teachers fear that forcing involvement may result in increasingly unfavorable attitudes. In a 1976–77 study of science attitudes, however, NAEP revealed that girls' participation levels may not reflect their attitudes. NAEP asked 9-year olds a series of questions which were phrased in two ways: Children were asked, "Would you like to . . ." (desired participation), and "Have you ever . . ." (actual participation) for the same activities (Kahle and Lakes, 1983). Girls' actual levels of participation were lower than their expressed desire to participate in many activities.

Girls often do not receive the encouragement that boys do. Instead, elementary teachers tend to react more favorably to boys. When these teachers are asked to identify scientifically talented or gifted students, a cross-cultural pattern emerges: They identify more boys. Furthermore, observation of both the number and duration of teachers' interactions with identified creative girls and boys revealed that teachers interact twice as often and for longer durations with boys, compared to girls. In England, M. G. Spear (1984) analyzed the markings of science papers attributed to 12-year-old boys and girls and found that both male and female science teachers generally gave higher marks when the work was attributed to a boy. In addition, different interaction patterns are found. Frequently, teachers allow boys to dominate discussions and the use of equipment, and they are four times more likely to select boys as target students than girls (Tobin and Garnett, 1987).

The elementary school as an institution also provides different educational experiences for girls and boys. Current institutional practices consistently use gender as the basis to group children when many other criteria are available.

As an alternative, school activities could be designated as quiet or adventurous with all students taking part in the different kinds of activities in the playground and the classroom. By ensuring equity in the corridors as well as in the classroom, schools would come much closer to providing optimal settings for science instruction.

Secondary School

Although equal numbers of boys and girls attend science classes in elementary and middle/junior high schools where enrollment is mandatory, in high school the situation changes. After age 14, the differences in out-of-school science experiences for boys and girls are exacerbated by different in-school science experiences (Kahle and Lakes, 1983). Although equal numbers of boys and girls take high-school biology, only 30 percent of high-school girls, compared with 39 percent of boys, take chemistry. Physics, taken by 26 percent of all high-school boys, is studied by only 14 percent of the girls.

Furthermore, the ratio of male-to-female science students is reflected in the ratio of male-to-female science teachers. In the United States, only 24 percent of secondary-school science teachers are women, and the majority of them teach biology (Weiss, 1978). Without role models, girls may feel less comfortable or more out-of-place in upper-level science courses.

The decline in the number of girls continuing on in physical science courses (chemistry and physics) has been attributed to many causes: lack of interest, lack of aptitude, and science and/or math anxiety. In addition, both curricula and teaching styles may affect enrollment patterns of boys and girls in elective science courses.

In hopes of increasing the appeal of science to women and minorities, the publishing industry has increased pictorial representations of female and minority populations. Publishing guidelines ensure that segments of our population are represented pictorially in correct proportions, and therefore, books now have approximately 50 percent of illustrations and diagrams showing females and 17 percent depicting Blacks. While these cosmetic changes are a beginning, textbooks still need substantive changes. For example, in the 1985 editions of two popular high-school biology texts, between 75 percent and 98 percent of the cited scientific work described the contributions of men, while the texts cited the contributions of women as only 2 percent and 4 percent of the total. In spite of the changes thus far, woman's role in science still seems minimal and uninviting for young girls today.

Teaching styles also may affect enrollment patterns. In 1981, M. Galton identified three different styles in science teachers: problem solvers, informers, and enquirers. The *problem solver* teacher uses many questions and a low frequency of pupil-initiated and maintained activities; the *informers* primarily use teacher delivery of facts and infrequently use questions except to recall facts; and *enquirers*, who use pupil-initiated and maintained experiments as well as inferring, formulating, and testing hypotheses. Generally, girls prefer the latter style of teaching, the enquirers. It comes as no surprise that this is the style most often used in biology classes, which girls often select. In contrast, the problem-solver strategy is least favored by girls, and it is more frequently used in physics, which few girls elect to study. In addition, female teachers more commonly use the enquiry style, while men favor the informer or problem-solver mode of instruction (Douglass, 1985). Could the different teaching styles influence girls away from physics and chemistry?

Classroom ethnographers also divide science instruction into several other categories: whole-class (lecture/demonstration), whole-class interactive (discussion), small group (laboratory), and individual (seat work/projects). Girls and boys respond differently to these various modes of instruction, yet overwhelmingly teachers use the whole-class mode. For example,

L. Trowbridge and R. Bybee (1987) report that high-school teachers lecture over 70 percent of instructional time, and K. Tobin's (1987) research in the United States and in Australia indicates that the vast majority of secondary teachers studied (29 out of 33 in his studies) primarily use whole-class instruction. Tobin reports certain differences in teachers' interactive patterns with boys, as opposed to girls, during whole-class instruction.

> Teachers tended to involve males and females to an equal extent in lower cognitive level interactions, but tended to involve males to a greater extent than females in higher cognitive level interactions. Males also participated in a more overt way than females by volunteering to respond to teacher questions by raising their hands when teachers asked questions in a whole-class setting. The major consequence of this engagement pattern was that "target" males were involved in responding to questions intended to stimulate thinking or to elicit responses that would provide a bridge to a new area of content. . . . The pattern of male students being more involved than females in whole-class interactions was apparent in classes taught by male and female teachers. (p. 39)

Tobin and others have found similar patterns in classes that are tracked on science ability and in ones that are elected by advanced students. For example, in one eleventh-grade biology class which contained 12 girls and 9 boys, approximately 70 percent of teacher questions were answered by boys. In all cases, the observed teachers invariably claimed that they involved girls and boys equally.

Tobin (1987) reports few gender differences in teacher-student interaction patterns during individualized activities; however, gender differences still occur during laboratory activities and in the classroom. Tobin, concurring with J. Whyte (1986), reports that boys tend to dominate the equipment as well as the activities. Whyte concludes that "boys are pushier and seem to regard scientific or technical resources as rightfully theirs. Girls, for their part, become unwilling to enter into an undignified scrabble for equipment" (p. 34). As noted, boys are also asked more higher-order cognitive questions than are girls (Tobin and Garnett, 1987; Tobin and Gallagher, 1987). In the classroom, teachers act differently toward boys and girls. Boys are urged to "try harder" when they do not succeed (Sadker and Sadker, 1985). When giving instructions for completing a problem, teachers give boys specific instructions, while they may show girls how to finish a task or do it for them. They subtly convey to students that boys have the ability to succeed in science and mathematics, but girls do not. A recent study suggests that this non-verbal message may account for a large portion of the gender differences observed in science achievement, since it causes girls to lose self-confidence in their scientific ability. Does the "I don't know" response, discussed at the article's beginning, reflect this lack of self-confidence? Linn and her co-workers found that in a study involving 13- and 17-year olds, girls tend to use the "I don't know" response, particularly for physical-science items or for items with masculine references. They reported that gender-related differences in responses are due to lack of confidence and to differences in prior instruction (Linn et al., 1987). Teacher behavior, therefore, has an important effect on confidence levels as well as on achievement levels.

As noted previously, girls, compared with boys, have fewer verbal exchanges with teachers. This pattern continues even after teachers are sensitized to the difference. For example, S. Hyde (1986) reports that although one of her primary goals was to interest girls in physics, when her student-teacher interaction patterns in her classes were recorded, they show that she still spent 82 percent of her time with boys. What happened? One subtle possibility is that even though some teachers learn to monitor their verbal behavior patterns, they may continue to nonverbally communicate different expectations. For example, studies document that teachers use the following strategies to indicate anticipation of a superior performance: leaning forward, looking into eyes, nodding, and smiling. Do girls receive these non-verbal cues of anticipation?

The critical problem with different expectations is that they are group based, and therefore achievement expectations become a function of one's sex. Because students cannot change their gender, they accept the achievement expectation as something they cannot change. Therefore, different teacher expectations for boys and girls in certain subjects (for example, science and reading) contribute to the cultural expectations from different biological sexes and lead to a gender difference. For example, J. A. Rowell (1971) reports that teachers who expected girls to have difficulty learning physics had girls who did not perform as well as boys—a well-documented gender difference. However, no achievement differences were found between girls and boys who were enrolled in physics classes taught by teachers who did not hold such views. Clearly, teachers can either contribute to or detract from the achievement of girls in science.

Colleges and Universities

S. E. Berryman (1983) has shown that the attrition of women from science increases near the end of their education; that is, during the undergraduate and graduate years. Only 14 percent of the women entering college intend to major in science or engineering, compared to 40 percent of male freshmen (Vetter, 1987).

Despite increases in the numbers of women majoring in science and engineering during the 1970s, some areas peaked in 1984 and have begun to decline. For example, the percentage of women receiving a bachelor's degree in math, computer science, or statistics fell from 4.4 percent in 1986 to 2.4 percent in 1989 (in actual numbers from 20,400 to 9,600) (Vetter, 1987). Furthermore, a higher proportion of both undergraduate and graduate women, compared with men who elect a scientific course of study, chose to leave it before receiving a degree (Matyas, 1986; Hite, 1983).

Recently, several researchers have assessed the factors which lead to higher attrition rates for women, compared with men, from college science majors. N. C. Ware and V. Lee (1987) have summarized the research and identified six factors.
• Girls complete fewer high-school courses in science and math than boys.
• Girls demonstrate less quantitative ability as evidenced by the math section of the Scholastic Aptitude Test.
• Girls have lower self-estimates of their mathematic and scientific abilities.
• Girls perceive discrepancies between personality characteristics associated with femininity and those associated with scientists.
• Girls' parents have lower aspirations for them than boys' parents.
• Women in college tend to react more negatively to initial college courses in mathematics and science than comparable men.

Only one of the factors identified by Ware and Lee relates to academic ability or to a gender-related cognitive difference; that is, the lower average scores of girls, compared to those of boys, on the math section of the SAT. More recent studies, however, indicate that the average difference in girls' and boys' quantitative SAT scores is directly related to the number of math and math-related courses taken in high school rather than innate ability (LeBold, 1987). Ware and Lee analyzed the *High School and Beyond* data for college science majors. They found that high-school counselors and teachers positively influenced boys to take math and science but negatively influenced girls to do so, thus contributing to girls' lower math scores on the SAT.

Ware and Lee also found that personal and social factors, rather than academic ones, often influenced women against college science majors. They report that "concern for future family and personal life seem to inhibit the choice of a science major for females, but facilitate a science major for males" (p. 20). In other words, only social factors have been identified as contributing to the high attrition rate of women from college science and math courses. No academic or cognitive factors have been found.

Current studies focus on the personal factors which influence many talented women to drop college science majors. In A. L. Gardner's (1986) study, she asked female students in engineering, biology, and nursing to complete a Personal Attributes Questionnaire on which they rated themselves according to masculine and feminine characteristics. She found that only 18.5 percent of the women engineers and 23 percent of the women biologists, compared with 42 percent of the women nursing students, rated themselves as typically feminine. The majority of the female engineering and biology students (62 percent and 64 percent), respectively, selected characteristics which classified them as either masculine or androgynous. Those classifications required high self-ratings on characteristics such as self-confidence and tenacity. However, P. Newton (1986) found that young women enrolled in engineering courses in Britain stressed the feminine aspects of their personalities, perhaps in order to appear to be less different or unusual than women in other courses. The effect of women's self-perceptions on enrollment in and commitment to science and engineering majors needs to be assessed further.

Another factor influencing the high attrition rate of women from science at the college level might be inequities in the classroom. Researchers, skilled in assessing classroom climates, have noted small differential behaviors (micro-inequities) that often occur in the course of everyday exchanges in which individuals are singled out or ignored because of sex. In the classroom, teachers react differently toward their female students than toward their male students. Each incident is trivial, but the cumulative effect maintains unequal treatment based upon a personal characteristic which cannot be changed. Consider the following example:

> "Michelle," Professor Jones announces to his mechanical engineering class, "received the highest mark on the test. Her work is truly impressive and should be a challenge to the rest of you—especially you men."

The unrecognized, but voiced, micro-inequities include:
• the uniqueness of Michelle's achievement
• the challenge to increase competitiveness
• the question if "real men" will allow a woman to win

However, Michelle, herself, is probably pleased with the praise she has received. Only later will she become uncomfortable with some of its probable outcomes. For example, she may be kidded about her grades by the men and that kidding may question her femininity, or she may be excluded from a cooperative learning situation so that she doesn't "set the curve" the next time. The effect of micro-inequities on the choice of and perseverance in science by college women is a continuing and, often, unrecognized problem.

Proposing Solutions

Rather than propose untested solutions, I shall describe the results and promises of current research. The studies span the ages from 9-year olds to 20-year olds, covering science classes from grade school through college. The problem addressed by each is the recruitment and retention of female students in science courses and careers. Beyond recruitment and retention, however, each study focuses on equitable science education in which girls as well as boys participate at high cognitive levels in science classes.

J. B. Kahle (1985) identified and observed biology teachers in the United States who were successful in motivating tenth-grade girls to elect optional physics and chemistry courses. Selected teachers from Maine to California were observed, parents and principals were interviewed, and past and present students were surveyed. Approximately 395 children from varied backgrounds participated in the study, which provided a composite picture as well as a collective pool of data from which commonalities could be identified and generalizations made. It was found that the identified teachers taught in a more individualized way, using many discussions, as well as project and laboratory work. In addition, compared with a national sample control group (Weiss, 1978), they also used more diverse media, field trips, and library research.

In these teachers, researchers found three common practices which were easily applicable in all science teaching. First, teachers who were successful in encouraging students to continue in science quizzed or tested their students once a week. Second, they encouraged creativity, noted by 58 percent of boys and 67 percent of girls; and, third, they fostered basic skill development, according to over 70 percent of both boys and girls surveyed. The researchers also noted that these teachers emphasized skills using quantitative methods, transforming data, interpreting graphs, and visualizing three-dimensional objects (Kahle, 1985). These skills add both to the cognitive development and problem-solving skills of adolescents. The implementation of a science curriculum which develops creativity and originality while fostering cognitive growth would encourage and enable more girls, as well as more boys, to study science.

Studies which have analyzed teacher behaviors suggest that both male and female science teachers need to practice what S. M. Malcolm (1983) calls "directed intervention," in which all students are actively and positively encouraged to participate, respond, and question. If, as A. Kelly (1985) suggests, gender differentiation is maintained by the behavior of the children themselves, rather than teacher behavior, directed intervention may be one of the best ways to improve the cognitive development of girls.

Kelly, Whyte, and B. Smail had a similar goal in their 1984 study in England. The Girls in Science and Technology (GIST) project involved ten comprehensive schools in the Manchester area and studied 2,000 children from the time they entered lower school (age 11) until they made their subject choices at age 14. Based on observations and results, the research team suggested a prototype curriculum and hypothesized about ideal situations in middle/junior high school.

In its search for an ideal curriculum, the GIST project developed and tested new curricula as part of its four-year study; that is, when the teacher-participants requested new or different materials, they were developed. Designed to appeal to all students, particularly to girls, the curricular materials have the following characteristics:

- focuses on relationships as well as rules
- focuses on people as well as machines
- develops a pragmatic rather than a dogmatic approach
- views the world as a network rather than a hierarchy of relationships
- emphasizes the aesthetic as well as the analytical aspects of science
- focuses on nurturing living beings as well as on controlling inanimate things (Smail, 1984, p. 27)

The GIST project proposes the integration of the contributions of female scientists into the curriculum. Many associations such as the National Science Teachers Association can provide references and resources identifying the contributions of female scientists. In addition, GIST stresses the inclusion of "tinkering" activities in school science in order to overcome the lack of such experiences by girls in everyday life. The results of both the GIST project and Kahle's (1985) study demonstrate that the ideal secondary-science curriculum must provide experiences rotating three-dimensional figures in space, drawing and conceptualizing three-dimensional forms, and projecting curvilinear distances and outcomes. Such experiences increase a child's visual-spatial ability. Since girls usually have less experience with the toys, games, and activities which enhance spatial ability, opportunities must be constructed in the curriculum. The GIST project reveals that although boys initially score better on spatial-ability tests, enrolling girls in one technical-craft course eradicates the gender difference (Kelly et al., 1984).

Teachers and researchers concur that extensive laboratory work must be included in the curriculum to equalize the science educations of girls and boys. Laboratory activities can also be used to improve interest and experience in unfamiliar subjects. Perhaps a 15-year-old girl in Louisiana described the interest aspect best when she said, "I enjoy working with microscopes. We had a cow heart and we opened it up. [We] looked in the microscope at the different parts of the inside of the heart and I enjoyed that" (Kahle, 1985, p. 54).

The need for experience with the actual tools and techniques of science is well documented. Boys and girls both express anxiety if they do not have sufficient past experience against which to gauge success. For example, Kahle found that girls express little anxiety about focusing a microscope with which they have had experience but great anxiety about wiring an electric circuit with which they have had none. Similarly, boys express concern about taking the temperature of a living organism, a technique with which they are generally unfamiliar. In order to encourage girls to participate equally in science, an ideal curriculum would present alternative and supplementary materials familiar to girls. By providing examples and models drawn from the common experiences of girls (sewing machines and volleyball) as well as those of boys (cars and football), strides can be made toward equality.

In many countries, definitive studies have shown that experience makes the difference; that is, boys and girls express similar interest in topics with which they both have had experience (Kahle, 1985; Smail, 1985; Parker, 1985). Therefore, both curricula and instructional modes must allow for experiences with the equipment and instruments of science. Such experience may improve the problem-solving abilities of all students and contribute to cognitive development and understanding.

Teacher behavior can also affect student attitude. In a classic experiment conducted by Rennie, Parker, and P. E. Hutchinson (1985) in Western Australia, their results support the efficacy of changing teaching behaviors to effect changes in student attitudes. The researchers provided one set of elementary teachers with intensive training in the skills of teaching electricity as well as with information about non-sexist teaching, while a comparable group received only the skills training. They found "a slight but consistent tendency for students in the Experimental Group classes to perceive girls as more competent with electricity than did students in Control Group classes" (Parker, 1985, p. 12). When they asked the year-five children if they could become electricians, 90 percent of the boys in both the experimental and control classes responded positively, while 85 percent of the girls in the experimental group said "yes" compared to only 70 percent of the girls in the control group (Parker, 1985). The behavioral training the teachers received made a tremendous difference in the attitudes of both the class as a whole and the girls, themselves.

One way of making classroom climates more favorable for girls' cognitive development has been proposed by a Norwegian project. The researcher/teacher observation team for fourth- through sixth-grade science lessons suggests the following change in methodology, which has encouraged more participation from girls in the question/answer sessions with teachers. In the usual classroom presentation, teachers begin a lesson by asking pupils what they know about a topic, and boys answer the majority of the questions based on knowledge from experiences outside the classroom which generally their female counterparts have never had. Instead, if pupils begin the activity at once, with little introduction from the teacher, everyone has access to the experience. A discussion by the teacher after the activity, rather than before, encourages more participation by girls (Jorde and Lea, 1987).

Kahle's (1985) study, discussed earlier, also proposes another means for creating better classroom climates for girls by providing a pleasant, attractive, and stimulating environment for learning science. While the study's pleasant surroundings and activity-initiated lessons provided a relaxed and less competitive atmosphere for studying science, girls' performance levels remained unaffected. Kahle had hoped to increase the girls' interest and performance levels by providing information, female role models, and interest-oriented curricular materials. The project, however, produced limited results. When assessments of students' science achievement, interest, and attitudes were made after the project, it was found that boys, as compared to girls

- had more experiences in science
- indicated higher interest in science careers
- held more positive perceptions of science and scientists
- expressed more positive attitudes toward science and scientists
- found science more useful
- received significantly more A and B grades in science (Kahle, 1987)

The indirect, interest-oriented approach may have improved the biology classroom climate for girls, but it failed to increase the cognitive-achievement levels or to improve the science attitudes of girls. Activities or curricula focused on interests and careers may temporarily encourage girls as well as boys to participate in science, but they will not expand girls' horizons or improve their skills in science. In order to change classroom climates as well as student attitudes and achievement levels, intervention activities must be direct, explicit, and capable of sustaining girls' interest in science. But prerequisite skills must be provided, or girls will lag behind boys in achievement levels and attitudes. Rigorous science experiences and skill development are an essential part of an effective classroom climate.

Rennie et al.'s (1985) study, conducted in elementary schools in Western Australia, combined rigorous skill training with activities designed to improve the classroom climates. They found that more time was spent in group work, and more girls actively participated in the experimental activities after the training sessions. The science classes, therefore, had become more equitable, and the climate had improved for girls.

At the college level, changes in the campus climate are likewise necessary to improve the entrance and retention of women in science. Micro-inequities, as discussed earlier, are usually regarded as a classroom problem, but the atmosphere of the campus may also affect women's selection of non-traditional majors. In a 1986 study, M. L. Matyas assessed the overall campus climates which may affect the attrition of women from college science majors. She compared women and men who were switching from a biology major to other majors and found that the women had higher grade-point averages than the men. The women were capable of the science and mathematics required, but some other factor had motivated the change in major. Matyas found that personal factors often affected the decisions. While some of the personal factors related to future concerns, others related to both campus and classroom climates; for example, a lack of role models, a lack of female friends in a science major, and a male orientation in science.

Many college women in non-traditional majors, therefore, may feel isolated. In W. K. LeBold's (1987) study, he suggests that a "critical mass" of any group is necessary before members of that group feel comfortable in a given situation. "However, when a critical mass is reached, many of the socialization problems are minimized, women recognize that there are others 'in the same boat,' and the resulting self-support groups are eventually institutionalized" (p. 86). LeBold suggests programs that are successful in increasing the number of women in non-traditional fields must address at least four issues: recruitment, retention, future employment, and program evaluation. Furthermore, he warns that fragmented programs, focusing on a single issue, often are ineffective. In addition, LeBold states that single-issue programs may delete or delay any concerted effort to improve classroom or campus climates for women. Rather, a single program may be used to justify the lack of the coordinated, sustained effort needed.

Summary

For over a decade research has focused on the scarceness of women in science. The research has analyzed personal, societal, and educational factors. Data have been collected and statistically analyzed, and yet, the situation has not improved. Girls, in comparison to boys, still do not perform as well on cognitive items in the NAEP's science survey, on the mathematics section of the SAT, and on the Second International Educational Assessments in Science.

Yet, with intervention programs based on current research, teachers can favorably affect the attitudes and achievement levels of diverse students in science. Spatial-visual activities, basic skill development, and tinkering with and testing equipment, as well as frequent tests will help all children progress in science. As more girls succeed and continue in science, a critical mass will be prepared for college science majors. Eventually, more girls will eagerly respond, "Yes, I know" to questions on national and international assessments of science knowledge and skills.

References

Berryman, S. E. (1983, November). *Who will do science?* Washington, DC: The Rockefeller Foundation.

Douglass, C. B. (1985). Discrepancies between men and women in science: Results of a national survey of science educators. In J. B. Kahle (Ed.), *Women in science.* Philadelphia: The Falmer Press.

Galton, M. (1981). Differential treatment of boy and girl pupils during science lessons. In A. Kelly, (Ed.), *The missing half.* Manchester: Manchester University Press.

Gardner, A. L. (1986). *Effectiveness of strategies to encourage participation and retention of precollege and college women in science.* Unpublished doctoral dissertation, Purdue University, West Lafayette, IN.

Harlen, W. (1985). Girls and primary-school science and higher education: Sexism, stereotypes and remedies. *Prospects, 15*(4), 541–551.

Hite, L. M. (1983). *A study of doctoral students compared by gender and type of field of study on factors of role congruence, perceived support from faculty, and perceived support from peers.* Unpublished doctoral dissertation, Purdue University, West Lafayette, IN.

Hyde, S. (1986). Girls and science—Strategies for change. *Pivot, 3,* 28–30.

Iliams, C. (1985). Early school experiences may limit participation of women in science. In J. C. Craig and J. Hardings, (Eds.), *Contributions to the third GASAT conference* (pp.79–85). London: Chelsea College, University of London.

Johnston, S. (1984). Girls need a science education too. *The Australian Science Teachers Journal, 30*(2), 18–23.

Jorde, D., and Lea, A. (1987). The primary science project in Norway. In J. B. Kahle, J. Z. Daniels, and J. Harding (Eds.), *Proceedings of fourth GASAT conference* (pp. 66–72). West Lafayette, IN: Purdue University.

Kahle, J. B. (1985). Retention of girls in science: Case studies of secondary teachers. In J. B. Kahle (Ed.), *Women in science.* Philadelphia: The Falmer Press.

Kahle, J. B. (1987). SCORES: A project for change? *International Journal of Science Education, 9*(3), 325–333.

Kahle, J. B., and Lakes, M. K. (1983). The myth of equality in science classrooms. *Journal of Research in Science Teaching, 20*(2), 131–140.

Keller, E. F. (1986). How gender matters: Or why it's so hard for us to count past two. In J. Harding (Ed.), *Perspectives on gender and science* (pp. 168–183). London: The Falmer Press.

Kelly, A., Whyte, J., and Smail, B. (1984). *Final report of the GIST project.* Manchester: Manchester University, Department of Sociology.

Kelly, A. (1985). The construction of masculine science. *British Journal of Sociology of Education, 6*(2), 133–153.

LeBold, W. K. (1987). Women in engineering and science: An undergraduate research perspective. In L. S. Dix (Ed.), *Women: Their underrepresentation and career differentials in science and engineering* (pp. 49–98). Washington, DC: National Academy Press.

Linn, M. C., de Benedictis, T., Delucchi, K., Harris, A., and Stage, E. (1987). Gender differences in national assessment of education progress science items: What does "I don't know" really mean? *Journal of Research in Science Teaching, 24*(3), 267–278.

Malcolm, S. M. (1983, July). *An assessment of programs that facilitate increased access and achievement of females and minorities in K–12 mathematics and science education.* Washington, DC: American Association for the Advancement of Science, Office of Opportunities in Science.

Matyas, M. L. (1986, May). *Persistence in science-oriented majors: Factors related to attrition among male and female students.* Paper presented at American Educational Research Association, San Francisco, CA.

Mullins, I., and Jenkins, L. (1988). *The science report card. Elements of risk and recovery* (Report no.: 17–S–01). Princeton: Educational Testing Service.

Newton, P. (1986). Female engineer: Femininity redefined? In J. Harding (Ed.), *Perspectives on gender and science* (pp. 40–61). London: The Falmer Press.

Parker, L. H. (1985, Dec.). *Non-sexist science education: An issue of primary concern.* Paper presented at the Science Teachers Association of Victoria Conference, Monash University, Melbourne, Australia.

Parker, L. H., and Rennie, L. J. (1986). Sex-stereotyped attitudes about science: Can they be changed? *European Journal of Science Education, 8*(2), 173–183.

Rennie, L. J., Parker, L. H., and Hutchinson, P. E. (1985). *The effect of inservice training on teacher attitudes and primary school science classroom climates.* (Research Report No. 12). Perth: University of Western Australia.

Rowell, J. A. (1971). Sex differences in achievement in science and the expectations of teachers. *The Australian Journal of Education, 15*(1), 16–29.

Sadker, D., and Sadker, M. (1985). Is the ok classroom, ok? *Phi Delta Kappan, 66*(5), 358–361.

Sjoberg, S. (1986). *Naturfag og Norsk Skole* (trans. Science and the Norwegian school). The National Report of the Second International Educational Assessment in Science Study. Oslo: University of Oslo.

Smail, B. (1984). *Girl-friendly science: Avoiding sex bias in the curriculum.* London: Longman.

Smail, B. (1985). An attempt to move mountains: The 'girls into science and technology' (GIST) project. *Journal of Curriculum Studies, 17*(3), 351–354.

Spear, M. G. (1984). Sex bias in science teachers' ratings of work and pupil characteristics. *European Journal of Science Education, 6*(4), 369–377.

Tobin, K. ,(1987). Gender differences in science: They don't happen here! In B. Fraser and G. J. Giddings (Eds.), *Gender issues in science education,* (Monograph No. 8) (pp. 37–45). Perth: Curtin University of Technology, Faculty of Education.

Tobin, K., and Gallagher, J. J. (1987). The role of target students in the science classroom. *Journal of Research in Science Teaching, 24,* 61–75.

Tobin, K. and Garnett, P. (1987). Gender differences in science activities. *Science Education, 71*(1), 91–105.

Trowbridge, L., and Bybee, R. (1987). *Becoming a secondary school science teacher,* (4th ed.). Columbus, OH: Merrill Publishing Co.

Vetter, B. M. (1987). Women's progress. *Mosaic, 18*(1), 2–9.

Ware, N. C., and Lee, V. (1987). *Sex differences in the choice of college science.* Unpublished paper, Radcliffe College, Cambridge, MA.

Weiss, I. R. (1978). *Report of the 1977 National survey of science, mathematics, and social studies education* (Report SE78–72). Washington, DC: U.S. Government Printing Office.

Whyte, J. (1986). *Girls into science and technology.* London: Routledge and Kegan Paul.

Graphs, Graphing, and Graphers

Heather M. Brasell

Coffee High School
Douglas, Georgia

Of all our means of transmitting information, graphs are unique in the variety and amount of information they convey. Graphs are powerful as a visual display of quantitative information (Tufte, 1983), and they are particularly effective in communicating relationships. They can convey vast amounts of information that cannot be communicated effectively by words or numbers alone. Graphs are a powerful and flexible medium for a wide variety of tasks, from describing data and revealing relationships to communicating comparative results. We can extract salient features quickly or focus on details. In short, graphs allow us to see the leaves (specific details or data analysis), the branches (relationships or data synthesis), or the whole tree (underlying structure of ideas or data integration) (Bertin, 1983), depending on our interests and needs. This ability of graphs to operate on three levels makes graphing an essential communication tool.

Graphs in Practice

The Power and Purpose of Using Graphs. Compared with verbal language, graphs are an information-dense system. They condense and distill a lot of information into a small space. A well-designed graph often displays information that would otherwise take several paragraphs to describe. For instance, the climatic diagram format in Figure 1 is widely used to summarize climatic data for a given location and to compare climatic information for different locations. The temperature and rainfall scales are carefully selected to indicate three ecologically important regions of the graph—wet, dry, and in between. We can see immediately the

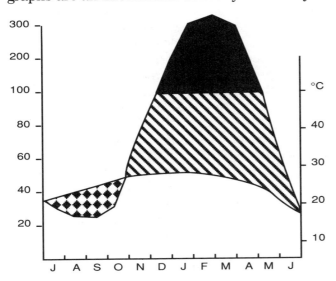

Figure 1. Climatic diagram for Atherton, Australia. Solid area (>100 mm) represents moisture surplus, while dotted area represents moisure stress.

extent and seasonal distribution of moisture surplus and stress. Yet, if we choose, we can also extract monthly temperature and rainfall data.

Graphs provide us with a variety of information, not just from the data points themselves, but also from other parts of the graph. Consider, for instance, the speed-time graph shown in Figure 2. The data points indicate the speed of an object at a given time. The slope of the line tangent to the curve at a given point represents the object's acceleration at that point, and the area bounded under the curve by any two points in time represents the distance traveled by the object. Although the ability of graphs to display this much varied information contributes to their power of communication, it is a difficult concept for students to grasp. This will be discussed in more detail later in this chapter.

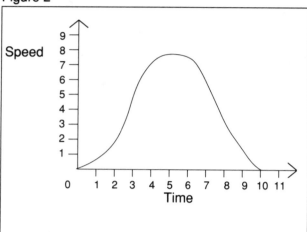

Figure 2

Graphs are also capable of data synthesis: They convey patterns, trends, and relationships in an easily recognizable format. Using graphs, the human brain generally out-performs the computer in detecting and analyzing patterns among spatially organized information. By facilitating pattern recognitions, a well-chosen graph is a powerful statistical and interpretive tool. The exposed patterns provide insight into the structure of information and help us to confirm or disprove expected behavior, discover new phenomena, or reveal causal and correlational relationships among variables. These patterns can be examined either quantitatively or qualitatively.

The Practice of Using Graphs. We use graphs in many areas of our life and work—biological and physical sciences; mathematics and statistics; applied science; social, financial, and governmental policy; and magazines and newspapers—to help us interpret quantitative information (MacDonald-Ross, 1977). While most of the contemporary formats of statistical graphs and charts were developed and refined by William Playfair about 1750–1800, the use of graphs and charts has recently blossomed as industrial and scientific advances have demanded appropriate ways of using, summarizing, and communicating quantitative information. However, in many cases, graphs have not been used with maximum efficiency or effectiveness. This has been due primarily to several factors: a general lack of understanding of the potential power of graphic communication, the widespread use of graphs simply as substitutes for tables, the perception among the consumer public of graphs as devices to *mis*represent, and the assumption among some communicators that graphs are devices for "showing the obvious to the ignorant" (Tufte, 1983).

Why should we use graphs in the face of these unfavorable factors when data can be summarized by other means: tables, statistics, and mathematical equations? Because these formats lack the visual properties of graphs. Much of the early research compared the effectiveness of various formats—tables, graphs, bar charts, pie charts, and texts—in communicating information. In spite of substantive flaws in the research, the results consistently demonstrated that different formats were effective for different purposes. Compiled from the research, Table 1 provides some guidelines for using the most appropriate display format. Because of the spatial organization of data, graphs have significant advantages over tables in interpolating and extrapolating (information *additional* to the data points themselves), integrating information, and interpreting trends and relationships.

Table 1	
Guidelines for Appropriate Information Display for Specific Tasks of Data Interpretation	
Purpose for Using Graph	Appropriate Graph Format
Representing proportions of a single entity	Pie chart
Comparing proportions of separate entities	Table, dot/bar chart
Representing specific quantities	Table
Comparing specific quantities	Table, dot/bar chart
Interpolating, extrapolating specific quantities	Graph
Integrating specific quantities	Histogram, graph
Interpreting trends, patterns	Dot/bar chart, graph
Interpreting correlational or causal relationships	Graph

In recent years, graphing has been undergoing a transformation as the computer revolutionizes our capacity to collect, manipulate, and display information in a graphic format. Previously, only graphic artists could construct graphs for publication, but now computers make it simple for virtually anyone to construct a variety of graphics from any given data set. Unfortunately, information is not always presented in the most appropriate graph format. Many magazines and newspapers use graphics widely, but their graphs often fail to communicate fundamental relationships among the data. Instead, they demonstrate the amazing graphic capabilities of the computer—what E. R. Tufte (1983) has described as the "We-Used-A-Computer-To-Build-A-Duck Syndrome." The inappropriate use of graphs (even in scientific research papers) has generated a wave of criticism and demands for graphic competency.

In spite of the tremendous interest in graphics during the last two decades, cognitive research has been slow to follow. Some of the ambivalence towards graphing research has resulted from the interdisciplinary nature of the skill. Although many researchers have been interested in graphs, no single discipline has assumed the direct research responsibility. Researchers in statistics, cartography, psychology, technical drawing, graphic arts, psychophysics, communication theory, computer science, and education have examined graphs and graphing skills from their specialized perspective (Schmid, 1983), but there have been few attempts to integrate and synthesize their findings.

Graphs in Science. Science is particularly rich in systems for symbolically representing information and ideas about how and why things relate to or interact with one another. Although graphs are important, they are only one of many systems of graphic representation in science. Other spatially organized systems include light-ray diagrams, circuit diagrams, and force diagrams in physics; life cycles, water cycles, and heredity charts in biology; and periodic tables and molecular-structure diagrams in chemistry.

Graphing is generally taught in science programs at the elementary level. Graphing skills are so basic that they are included in standardized tests for measuring science-process, logical-reasoning, and problem-solving skills at all educational levels. By the time students enter college, educators generally assume that students are competent in graphing, among other science-process skills. This assumption will be examined later in the chapter.

Even within the sciences, there are differences in the use of graphs. Natural-science journals use far more graphs than journals in mathematics or the social sciences. In the social sciences, economics, and business management, researchers often examine trends and patterns in demographic and financial information involving categorical variables (appropriate for display in charts), spatial variables (maps), or time (time-course graphs). Information in the natural sciences more often involves continuous variables other than time or space (called "relational graphs" by Tufte, 1983), and the purpose of graphing is more often to demonstrate the relationships among variables or derived information. Relational graphs account for a much higher proportion of total graphs used in high-school natural-science textbooks (77 percent in *Chemical Principles*, 48 percent in *The Project Physics Course*, and 18 percent in *Biological Sciences: An Ecological Approach*), than in social-science textbooks (no more than 5 percent) (Tufte, 1983). Similarly, among the graphs used in standardized tests at all levels from grade school through college, relational graphs account for 67 percent in natural science, 41 percent in mathematics, and only 24 percent in social sciences (Tufte, 1983).

Graphs in Theory

Visual Perception. As with any system for representing and communicating information, we attach meaning to graphs according to a set of rules or grammar. To read or interpret graphs, we must have at least an implicit understanding of this grammar. To construct graphs, however, we need more: Our understanding must be conscious and explicit.

Graph comprehension involves two processes: visual perception—the process of detecting the visual image of the graph, and graphic cognition—the process of converting this visual image into meaningful information (Kosslyn, 1985; Pinker, 1981). When reading and interpreting graphs, the process of graphic cognition is of primary concern. In contrast, graph construction requires an explicit understanding of the constraints and capabilities of both visual perception and graphic cognition in order to optimize the efficiency and effectiveness of a graphic display.

Visual perception is the process of visually detecting and discriminating among the separate elements of the graphic display and deriving visual (or semantic) meaning from their spatial organization. Research on human psychophysical factors has determined the minimum size for an element to be detected, the minimum size difference (as a proportion) for discriminating among separate elements, and the ability of the eye-brain system to quantify various visual properties such as size, orientation, shade, hue, intensity, and texture.

Our perceptions of some visual properties are systematically distorted. For instance, inappropriately scaling the axes can optically distort data; also, proximity to horizontal and vertical lines can systematically bias the perception of area. W. S. Cleveland and co-workers (Cleveland, 1985) have investigated a number of elementary graphic-perception tasks and ranked them as follows from most to least accurate in judgment:
• position along a common scale
• position along identical, non-aligned scales
• length
• angle or slope
• area
• volume

• color, hue, saturation, or density

This ranking provides an important principle guiding data display: Data should be encoded so that visual perception involves tasks as high on this scale as possible.

Graphic Cognition. Once a visual image has been received, it must then be converted to relevant information: the process of graphic cognition. S. Pinker (1981) has developed a theory of graph comprehension that synthesizes ideas from diverse sources, such as areas of information-processing psychology and artificial intelligence. This conceptual framework suggests that three main factors govern the process of extracting information from the visual display.

• An appropriate graph schema is essential for graphic cognition. In general, the schema embodies knowledge of what graphs are for, how they are interpreted, and the syntax or grammar of the graph.

• Selective attention is important because short-term or working memory is limited in capacity, retention, and rate of transfer of information to long-term memory. This is especially important for novice graph users who are unsure how to divide their attention.

• Salience, or the likelihood of a given element being noticed, will be influenced by innate attributions of the graph (e.g., dynamic display, color, shape, etc.) and by previous experience.

According to Pinker, a visual image enters the information-processing system via a sensory receptor (the eyes), which registers an array of marks or elements. Individual elements may be combined and encoded (chunked) as a single pattern with visual meaning (e.g., the line on the graph is increasing, decreasing, linear, or curve, etc.). In working memory, these patterns are given logical meaning by applying the appropriate grammar provided by the graph schema in long-term memory (e.g., profits are increasing; over time, volume expands as temperature increases; etc.). This grammar specifies how to link the graphic elements and the concepts (e.g., to quantify the data points). The graph schema specifies how to

- translate visual information in the graph into a conceptual message
- translate a conceptual question into a search strategy
- recognize which type of graph, complete with pertinent grammar, is appropriate (Pinker, 1981)

When we analyze a graph, we extract essential information in two fundamentally different ways—either by recognition (bottom-up processing) or by searching (top-down processing). This is the difference between looking at graphs and asking questions of them. Many tasks require a combination of recognition and search strategies.

In bottom-up encoding, elements in long-term memory appear to be automatically activated by the visual image itself—without requiring conscious attention or control, stressing capacity limitations of working memory, or interfering with other ongoing mental processes. This kind of automatic message assembly develops with practice in consistent matching of stimuli with responses.

Top-down encoding (or interrogation, or controlled search) either retrieves or encodes new information on the basis of conceptual questions (i.e., information that the reader wants to extract from the context). Searching behaviors may be induced by a number of factors: hypotheses, textual cues, and contextual purpose. These behaviors appear to require attention, be capacity-limited, and be done serially.

Graph Construction. Graph designers have to address explicitly three main concerns, in addition to the issues of graphic cognition

• selecting an appropriate graph format
• arranging information unambiguously in the graph
• designing the graph to enhance visual perception

This demands a combination and balance of substantive, statistical, artistic, and linguistic skills. If the artistic elements are allowed to dominate, graphs may have visual impact but be otherwise misleading, confusing, or ineffectual.

Because no single graphic format or design will prove universally superior for all sets of data and all purposes of communication (Table 1), no single algorithm for choosing format and design is likely to optimize the display. Instead of algorithms, graph construction must be guided by principles such as clear vision and clear understanding (Cleveland, 1985). The visual organization of the graph should correspond to the logical organization of the data. Tufte (1983) describes this eloquently in his principles of graphic excellence:

> Graphical excellence is the well-designed presentation of interesting data—a matter of *substance, statistics,* and *design.*
>
> Graphical excellence consists of complex ideas communicated with clarity, precision, and efficiency.
>
> Graphical excellence is that which gives to the viewer the greatest number of ideas in the shortest time with the least ink in the smallest space.
>
> Graphical excellence is nearly always multivariate.
>
> And graphical excellence requires telling the truth about the data. (p. 51)

Much of the designer's role is to make the information more immediate and reduce confusion. In addition to capitalizing on perceptual mechanisms and accommodating the working-memory constraints of the reader, the designer must use and conform to the visual grammar and syntax of the graph schema. Guidelines for constructing graphs are available in several "how-to" texts and manuals (e.g., Cleveland, 1985; Schmid, 1983; Tufte, 1983).

Graphs in Classrooms

The ability to use graphs (sometimes termed graphicacy, graphicity, graphic literacy, or visual literacy) is an important basic process skill. Along with literacy, numeracy, and articulateness, it is considered one of the basic intellectual skills (Balchin, 1972), each of which involves the ability to use and understand the conventions, rules, and grammar of a particular system for representing and exchanging information. Two major determinants of a student's performance in graphing are the competence of the student and the difficulty of the graphing task.

Complexity of Graph Format. Some features inherent in the graph format or the graphing task contribute to the level of difficulty in constructing or interpreting graphs. These difficulties increase with the number of variables represented in a graph. Although graphs are powerful for two-dimensional data, they become increasingly more difficult to use effectively as the number of data dimensions (variables) expands. Additional variables are frequently represented as multiple lines on the graph (e.g., Figure 1). Multiple dimensions of data are equally difficult to represent with text, tables, and other graphic representations. Although representations of concepts with algebraic equations are not so restrictive, most students find graphs more perceptually concrete and imaginable than equations.

Complex graph shapes are more difficult to interpret than simple ones. For instance, linear graphs are generally easier to interpret than curved ones. Visual perception capabilities allow most people to detect departures from linearity more reliably and accurately than departures from a smooth curve. The slope of curved graphs is also not immediately apparent—determination of the tangent to the curve is necessary. Logarithmic and exponential scales can be used to convert a curved graph to a linear one, but these scales are conceptually more difficult to interpret than natural scales.

Complexity of the Concept. The complexity of the concept is another factor which influences the difficulty in graph interpretations. Graphs of simple, measurable properties are considerably easier to interpret than graphs of more complex or abstract properties (e.g., rates, cumulative values, derived values [area, volume]) (Brasell, 1987). Consider, for example, the increasing abstractness of distance, velocity, and acceleration. Distance is a simple, familiar concept, measurable in units of length. Velocity can be derived as the ratio of distance to elapsed time (i.e., it is a "per" quantity, such as meters per second). Hence, velocity is more abstract and difficult to comprehend and graph. Acceleration is a ratio of velocity to time—a ratio of a ratio (i.e., it is a double "per" quantity, such as meters per second per second)—so it is even more conceptually difficult than velocity. Because velocity and acceleration are derived from distance and time data, all four variables can be represented simultaneously on the same two-dimensional graph (Figure 2). The height of the line at any point indicates the velocity of the object. The slope of the line, the ratio of velocity (the variable on the y-axis) and time (the variable on the x-axis), represents the object's acceleration. The total area under the curve, the product of the variable's velocity and time, represents the distance traveled by the object.

Because graphs can relate so many concepts simultaneously, graphs or features of graphs can sometimes generate some cognitive conflict with other cognitive structures or concepts (i.e., graphs can be counterintuitive). One example is the apparent inconsistency in the fact that the *distance* an object has traveled is represented on a velocity-time graph (Figure 2) as the *area* under the curve. Although this apparent inconsistency can be reconciled easily by considering the algebraic relationships between distance, time, and velocity, students seldom cross-check for consistency. Another example of a counterintuitive graph is the graph of data generated from an event that has a strong visual image associated with it. The mental image may be more visually compelling than the graph of the data. Inability to handle the cognitive discrepancy between the visual images of the event and the graph often results in the "graph-as-picture" misconception discussed below.

Representing negative quantities on graphs also causes difficulty. Although students usually have little experience with graphs of negative quantities, they do not have difficulty in constructing or reading graphs of negative *scalar* quantities, such as temperatures below zero or negative bank balances. With negative *vector* quantities, however, students often have problems because vector quantities simultaneously represent two separate attributes, direction and amount. For instance, most students of introductory college-level physics have considerable difficulty with graphs of negative velocity or force (Goldberg and Anderson, in press). Given an event in which a ball rolls up an inclined plane and then rolls back down (Figure 3a), students incorrectly assume that the slope of the velocity graph changes when the direction of motion changes instead of the correct graph (Figure 3b).

Figure 3

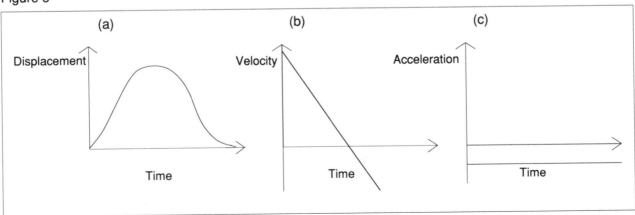

F. M. Goldberg and J. H. Anderson (in press) interpret these difficulties in two ways. First, the students seem to treat the entire graph as though it were positive, believing that a negative quantity simply implies a "lesser amount." Second, they fail to understand how one graph can provide information about two separate attributes (quantity and direction). They incorrectly assume that a change in the direction of motion requires a change in the direction of the line on the graph. Interpretation is frustrated by the apparent contradiction between a visual image (physically changing direction) and the graph of a straight line (no corresponding change).

Negative values of acceleration are even more counterintuitive and problematic. Students seem to associate negative acceleration with deceleration (i.e., slowing down), whereas an object with negative acceleration (Figure 3c) may be either speeding up (if velocity is also negative) or slowing down (if velocity is positive).

Complexity of the Task. As the complexity of the graphing task increases, the demand for top-down cognitive processing also increases. Comprehending most graphs requires that the reader relate information represented elsewhere—in another graph, a verbal description, a physical event, a data table, or an algebraic equation—to the graph before him. Three key factors determine the difficulty of establishing this relationship: the type of target information, the direction of the translation, and the conceptual distance between the two representations of the information.

In theory, any of the information resident in a graph may be decoded from it. In practice, however, some information is more readily accessible than other information, and this depends on both the visual and conceptual saliency of the information. For instance, the difficulty of obtaining specific quantitative information from the following graph features increases along the list: label, scale, data point, slope, area. Similarly, novice graphers are likely to have less difficulty determining specific information than with more general tasks, such as describing relationships, comparing graphs, identifying trends, or examining the underlying structure of ideas. The information-processing theory of graph comprehension (Pinker, 1981) does not adequately explain how these higher-order linkages are established and used.

The ease of translating from one format to another depends on the reader's comparative familiarity with the given formats. In a study in which high-school physics students were given items of equivalent content, they had a much higher error rate when translating from a verbal description to a graph (mean error rate 72 percent) than when translating from a graph to a verbal description (mean error rate 42 percent). H. M. Brasell (1987) attributed this to their greater competence with verbal than with graphic representations and posed the analogy of translating between two languages. It is easier to translate from a less familiar language to a more familiar one than vice versa. Students need experience translating both to and from graphs.

In general, the greater the similarity between two representations of information, the easier it is to link them. The following list of systems for representing information constitutes a continuum of relatedness. The farther apart two systems appear in the list, the less related they are and the greater the difficulty in translating from one to another: graphs, tables, scientific text, colloquial text, spoken description, real-world physical event. A table is more similar to a graph than a spoken description, for example. In one study, equivalent written items differed only in how a real-world motion was described. High-school physics students had much higher error rates when motion was described in colloquial language (e.g., steady speed towards a detector) (mean error rate of 70 percent) than when it was described in mathematical-scientific language (e.g., constant negative velocity) (mean error rate of 43 percent) (Brasell, 1987). One reason for this difference may be that colloquial language conveys information that is more ambiguous, less focused, and provides fewer contextual cues than scientific terminology.

Measuring Graphing Skill. Because graphing skill is affected by the complexity of graph formats, concepts, and graphing tasks, students generally exhibit a range of graphing competence. In understanding and using a specific graphic representation, individuals may have three main types of difficulty.

• *Concepts.* They may not understand the variables or substantive concepts being graphed.

• *Grammar.* They may not know or be able to use the algorithms or grammar for encoding and decoding information in the graph.

• *Linkage.* They may not understand how to link the graph with the variables or with phenomena in the real world.

Several methods have been used to diagnose, examine, and measure students' graphing skills. Although there are many items that test graphing skills as a subset of science-process skills, few multiple-choice tests are designed specifically to measure graphing skills. One reason for this is the difficulty of separating knowledge of the concepts represented on graphs from facility with graphs as a system of representation. Another problem is the lack of the theoretical or empirical bases needed to construct a multiple-choice test for graphing skills or to validate the items. If such a test could be constructed, students' responses to test items could be examined for clues to weak components of graphing ability, problematic types of conceptual variables, and common misconceptions. In a multiple-choice format, however, over-tempting foils may entrap unwary students, and their wrong answers may not reflect a student's misconception accurately. There is also evidence that students make fewer errors when constructing their own graphs than when asked to select among several in a multiple-choice format.

Because graph-construction activities require explicit understanding of graphing conventions, they may be more useful than graph-interpretation tests for revealing foggy understanding of the functions and properties of graphs. The problem with this approach, however, is that objective graph-construction exercises are difficult to construct; both validity and reliability are likely to be low. Evaluation would also be difficult because graphs may be technically correct but still fail to use the graph features effectively. For instance, inappropriate selection of scales may result in a misleading graph or one that fails to reveal pertinent relationships. The reasons for various errors in construction may be ambiguous; thus graph-construction exercises may have more value as diagnostic tools than as normative measurement or research instruments.

Individual demonstration-interviews (discussed by McDermott, Rosenquist, and Van Zee, 1987; Mokros and Tinker, 1987), a variation of the clinical interview, can also be used to identify graphing difficulties. The investigator demonstrates a physical event to an individual student and then asks the student to perform a series of tasks, such as predicting and sketching the appropriate graph or reconstructing the event to reproduce a given graph. To probe the student's understanding, the investigator asks a series of structured questions, which may be expanded to clarify the student's response. Although this is not a practical tool for regular classroom use, the demonstration-interview technique is a useful research technique for identifying sources of difficulty with graphs and the concepts being graphed. The techniques can also be helpful in developing instructional strategies to overcome these difficulties.

Another qualitative approach to examining students' graphing skills is to compare the behavior of students who are competent with regard to graphing skills ("experts") and students whose graphing skills are inadequate ("novices") (e.g., Van Zee and McDermott, 1987). This is done using individual interviews where students "think aloud" as they apply their graphing skills in a series of tasks. Again, this technique is used primarily by researchers to diagnose and remedy difficulties. It can also be an effective classroom tutoring strategy.

Figure 4: *Student-Constructed Graphs, Representing Data from Five Trials Bouncing a Ball*

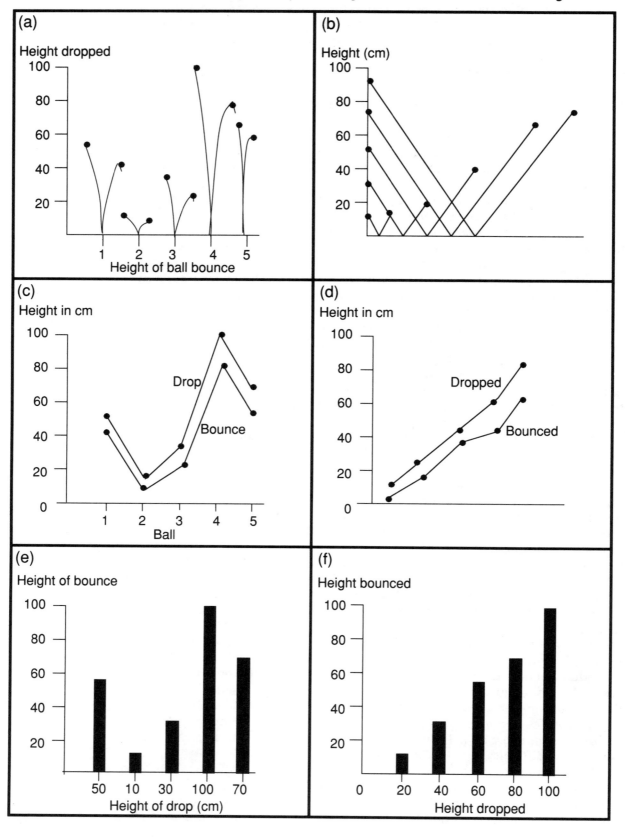

Researchers investigating graphing skills have consistently found fundamental deficiencies in students' graphing skills. Although the problems differ
in severity, students at different levels, from middle-school students (Mokros

and Tinker, 1987) to university students studying calculus-based physics (McDermott et al., 1987), have similar problems. They occur with a wide range of conceptual content. Graphing errors and misunderstandings are not restricted to students. Cleveland's (1984) survey of the graphs in leading scientific journals revealed that 30 percent of the articles contained a graphic error of some kind, either perceptual or cognitive.

As we analyze students' graphing skills, defining the level of skill in three broad categories of competence is helpful. At the most basic level, some students ("naive" graphers) do not understand the fundamental functions and properties of graphs. Students in the next category ("novice" graphers) understand only some of the functions and properties of graphs, and they perform satisfactorily on only the simplest of graphing tasks. Finally, a disappointingly small proportion of students can be considered competent ("expert" graphers).

Naive Graphers. Two kinds of misconceptions are common here. First, because graphs are a visual display, students may see them as a picture (called the "graph-as-picture" misconception). For instance, when these students are asked to select a graph to represent the speed of a person on a bicycle going up a hill, across the top, and down the other side, they produce a graph such as Figure 2, representing the shape of the hill rather than the speed. In actuality, the correct graph would be upside down from Figure 2 but otherwise would have the same general shape. That is, a cyclist would generally lose speed going up a hill and gain speed going down it.

Another example of the tendency to "picture" rather than graph a situation comes from a study in which high-school physics students constructed graphs to represent data for the drop height and rebound height of a bouncing ball (Brasell, 1987). Of 84 students, 18 produced graphs which represented both continuous variables (height of drop and height of bounce) on a single axis—the ordinate, or x-axis, (graphs a, b, c, and d in Figure 4). Half of these demonstrated the graph-as-picture misunderstanding (graphs a and b in Figure 4). Clearly these students did not understand the fundamental purpose of displaying the data in a graph.

As a third example, middle-school students were asked to construct a distance-time graph to represent the movement of an actor on a stage as he moved from left to right and returned. Some of them drew graphs that resembled the path of the actor, incorrectly representing time going backwards (called the "back-to-the-future" misconception) (Mokros and Tinker, 1987). Such a graph probably results from graphing the wrong variables (e.g., treating the time-course graph as a map-picture). It is also possible that the variables were plotted on the wrong axis.

Naive graphers do not understand that both axes of a Cartesian graph represent continuous variables. There is a tendency to treat data points along the x-axis as discrete units (i.e., categorical variables) as in bar charts (e.g., graphs e and f in Figure 4). This misunderstanding

Table 2		
Student Performance (Grades 7–12) on Each Category of the Test of Graphing Skills		
Graphing skill		(% maximum score)
Construction	plotting points	84
	assigning variables to axes	46
	scaling axes	32
	using best fit line	26
Interpretation	determining coordinates	84
	interpolating extrapolating	57
	describing relationships	49
	interrelating graphs	47

may account for many scaling errors in constructing graphs (e.g., Table 2, and graphs e and f in Figure 4) and for errors in interpolating and extrapolating (Table 2). In time-course graphs, students may represent an event where they see "nothing happening" (e.g., a stationary object) as a point on a time-course graph rather than as a continuous line. They fail to realize that time advances even when other variables remain the same.

Novice Graphers. Researchers have consistently found that most high-school and college students understand the elementary functions and properties of graphs in a superficial way—most are naive graphers. They often do not understand why graphs are used or how they can contribute to the processes of learning and communicating. Even when they understand the algorithms for determining coordinates, the mathematical relationships, and the variables represented (as tested by non-graph-based tests), students seem to perform satisfactorily only on tasks that involve direct reading of specific data from the graphs, that is, quantifying variables (e.g., Table 2).

One reason for the poor performance on more difficult graphing tasks may be that students commonly perceive graphs as equivalent to tables in displaying only specific data points. They seem to be unaware of other information resident in the slope, change of slope, or area of the graph, and they often fail to understand the meaning of the shape of the graph in describing how one variable relates to another. That is, they may understand the function of graphs in displaying and summarizing information but not appreciate the relational or mathematical properties of graphs or their power to synthesize and integrate information. Novice graphers have difficulty selecting the relevant features of a graph. Graphs have many distinguishable features (e.g., data points, lines, slopes, maxima, minima, points of inflection, changes of height, changes of slope, axes, scales, labels, captions), each of which contains a distinct part of the information represented. When students need to interpret a graph, often they are unsure which features are relevant to the specific task.

Novice graphers usually have two kinds of problems. First, students often do not know whether to obtain information from the slope or height of the graph. For instance, they construct a velocity-time graph that has the same shape as the distance-time graph and confuse velocity and acceleration graphs. Unless a student is interviewed, it is difficult to determine whether this problem represents a slope/height confusion (problems with graphs) or a velocity/distance (or acceleration/velocity) confusion (problems with the concept). In a recent study (Churchill and Goldberg, 1986), a college student clearly understood that the slope of a distance-time graph represents the velocity. However, she assumed that the area under the line of graph was the desired property, rather than the quantitative *value* of the slope.

Second, students commonly fail to understand the extent of information available in a graph. For instance, they seldom understand how to interpret the area under the line in a graph. Similarly, they fail to recognize quantities that cannot be determined from a graph. For example, they do not realize that it is impossible to tell an object's starting position from a velocity-time graph or whether an object is speeding up or slowing down from an acceleration-time graph (McDermott et al., 1987).

Students not only have difficulty selecting the relevant features of a graph but also fail to graph the relevant variables. Unless students are told which variable to plot on each axis, they are often unable to determine which variables from a data set are relevant to the task or how to assign the variables to the appropriate axes. Time is a particularly salient variable, perhaps because time-course graphs are so common. When constructing graphs, students often place time on the x-axis, regardless of the data set provided. For instance, in the graphs on the left in Figure 4, (graphs a, c, and e) students have organized the graph by the sequence of experimental data provided to them (hypothetical trial order, a pseudo-time variable) rather than exposing the fundamental relationships of the information.

Novice graphers also have difficulty relating a graph to another representation of the same information. Most students have difficulty relating information in a graph to the same or similar information presented in another format: relating one graph to another (e.g., constructing a velocity-time graph from a distance-time graph), matching verbal and graphic information (Table 2, describing relationships), integrating mathematical equations with graphic representations, and linking graphs with real-world variables or the physical phenomenon being represented in the graph (McDermott et al., 1987).

Expert Graphers. When novice graphers interpret a graph, they access and use a set of rules, or algorithms, which center on the simple principle that "greater quantities are indicated by 'more' of a mark (higher lines or bars, larger areas, etc.)" (Kosslyn, 1985, p. 509). With practice, expert graphers dispense with such explicit use of the rules and assign meaning to patterns of marks on the graph (i.e., increasing, decreasing, sigmoidal, etc.) (Kosslyn, 1985; Pinker, 1981). Expert graphers are then able to recognize a particular shape of graph as representative of a whole class of events. In this way, a cooling curve, a sigmoidal growth curve, or even a climatic diagram may be processed as a single "chunk" of information. The availability of such cognitive-graph templates is determined by familiarity.

Expert graphers appreciate the functions of graphs in synthesizing and integrating information, as well as in summarizing data. Competent graphers approach graphing tasks differently than novice graphers (Van Zee and McDermott, 1987). They selectively attend to axes (as reference points) and key features of the graph (indication of some change in at least one of the variables). They identify the dependent variable and visualize the way it changes with respect to the independent variable. They match the type of event with the shape of the graph (using cognitive templates) and check for consistency with alternative representations of the information. Nearly all of this behavior demands high-level cognitive processing of the graph information.

In summary, the main problem areas of students' graphing skills appear to be:

1. Facility with graphs is superficial, founded on algorithmic procedures rather than on a clear understanding of the graph's functions and its syntax.
2. Top-down processing of graphs is restricted to determining specific values (coordinates) of variables, even for graphs of simple variables. Fundamental relationships in graphs are seldom fully understood.
3. Lack of understanding of the function of graphs in synthesizing and integrating quantitative information is common. Two kinds of basic misunderstanding are apparent.
• Graphs may be seen pictorially.
• Graphs may be seen as equivalent to tabular information, ignoring information resident in the slope, change of slope, area, or general shape of the graph.

Which Students Have Difficulty. Unfortunately, students (and even many teachers) are not aware of their graphing deficiencies. In a recent study, 93 high-school physics students were asked about their attitudes towards graphs (Brasell, 1987). They generally thought graphs were useful but were indifferent about using them and seldom used them voluntarily. Only 12 of the students said they had difficulty either constructing or interpreting graphs. The students' subsequent performance, however, indicated that they greatly overestimated their graphing ability. This discrepancy might have been caused by their lack of previous experience with complex or challenging graphing tasks.

Because we lack adequate instruments for measuring graphing skills and research interest has only recently developed, it is not surprising that little is known about the influence of student attributes on graphing ability. Predictably, several studies show that graphing skills are correlated with various measures of general intelligence, ability, or reasoning and development. Several studies have also shown an increase in performance with age or grade level of students, probably resulting from increased experience and/or accompanying development, both of which are related to graphing abilities. These correlations, however, do not necessarily hold for all individuals. Several of the high-school physics students who produced the naive graphs in Figure 4 were above average in ability and development (Brasell, 1987). One had an SAT score of 1200. Conversely, Tufte (1983) describes seven-year-old Japanese children who have demonstrated competence with relational graphs. In short, the kind and nature of instructions and the opportunity for practice are probably important factors in developing graphical literacy.

Instructional Problems. Even with numerous graphing experiences in regular instruction, few students spontaneously develop graphing skills for different graph formats, types of contents, or different interpretation tasks. The rest flounder in uncertainty and resort to using limited algorithms, whether the algorithms are appropriate or not (e.g., Figure 4). Unfortunately, limited algorithms for reading and plotting coordinates are sufficient in many situations, so there is little incentive for students to apply themselves in mastering new skills.

Most of the formal instruction in graphing takes place within mathematics courses. Math concepts, such as proportional, inversely proportional, linear, exponential, are important in describing relationships among variables. Yet students do not automatically transfer these mathematical concepts to interpretation or construction of graphs in science (or other subjects). This may be largely due to overemphasis of a limited range of graph formats, conceptual content, and graphing tasks. Explicit instruction is often limited to routines for plotting and reading data points in simple graph formats. These algorithms work well for constructing graphs as part of laboratory reports as long as guidelines indicate which variables to plot on which axes. They are also sufficient for recognizing the appropriate graph in most multiple-choice graphing test items. However, the algorithms are not adequate for interpreting graphs or designing graph formats from raw data.

Instruction rarely includes graphs of negative quantities, vector variables, or more than two variables. Time-course graphs are so common that many students do not know how to handle other types of graphs. For instance, nearly all senior physics students would be able to calculate the area of a square given the length of the side. Yet, in one study, 59 percent of them were unable to select a graph with the correct shape to represent this relationship (Brasell, 1987).

Lab activities often require students to construct graphs. In most cases, however, the graphs are constructed directly from tables, reinforcing the notion that graphs are merely an alternative to tables as a means of representing numerical data. Students are seldom asked to use these graphs to draw conclusions or to construct hypotheses, so they come to see them as a superfluous appendix to the lab report, rather than as an integral part of understanding the phenomenon. Similarly, textbooks frequently present graphs as supplementary, nonessential information. Students can fulfill the requirements of most science courses without understanding the graphs they produce in their reports or the graphs that are shown in their textbooks. It is not surprising that students at all levels often skip the graphs in their textbooks.

In summary, because students typically experience only a limited range of graph formats and graphing tasks, they misunderstand the purpose of graphs, they underestimate the communicative potential of graphs, and they systematically overestimate their own graphing skills.

Instructional Strategies. If we want students to develop graphing skills, we need to teach these skills explicitly and directly. Instruction should provide students with experience in

- selecting appropriate graph features (i.e., coordinates, slope, change of slope, area, etc.)
- using similar graph formats in different contexts (templates)
- using graphs other than time-course
- translating information from graphs to concepts or events, as well as translating from events to graphs
- linking information in graphs with information elsewhere (tables, equations, text, real world) (McDermott et al., 1987)

Experience with graphing activities improves graphing skills (measured by multiple-choice tests), whether the activities are demonstration-discussion, simulation, hands-on laboratory, or microcomputer-based laboratories. However, researchers who are concerned with the students' misconceptions of graphs and the quality of their performance (assessed by individual interviews) maintain that students can only develop an appropriate graph schema and linkages between graph, concept, and real-world phenomena in labs where they generate their own data and graphs.

Microcomputer-based labs (MBLs) automate the procedures of collecting data and constructing graphs, and they have also proven very effective in improving graphing skills (Brasell, 1987; Linn, Layman, and Nachmias, 1987; Mokros and Tinker, 1987; Nachmias and Linn, 1987). Several features contribute to their effectiveness.

1. Many of the computer programs allow or encourage students to alter the parameters of the graph, such as the scale and label, and to compare graphs of different data. In this way, students learn the elements of graph construction without having to draw their own graphs.

2. Typical activities include predicting the graph for a particular physical event and designing a physical event to produce a given graph. Discrepancies between student predictions and the actual outcomes reveal misconceptions about either the graph or the concept. By directly confronting these misconceptions, students learn about the fundamental properties of graphs and concepts.

3. Real-time graphing, made possible by computers, helps to make the abstract properties being graphed behave as though they were concrete and manipulable. Displaying a graph at the same time as the real-world event generating the data helps students establish a cognitive link between them. A delay as short as 20 seconds in displaying the graph inhibits the development of this linkage (Brasell, 1987).

In contrast, students in conventional activities often forget the details of the lab activity by the time they construct the graph. The more direct the functional connections (in concept, experience, and time) between graphs and concepts or real-world events, the more likely it is that students will generate cognitive linkages and the more likely that they will appreciate the functions of graphs.

Experience with activities that cannot be completed by using simple algorithms also helps students realize the inadequacy of their graphing skills and encourages them to develop these skills. Activities that require students to ask questions of graphs by interpreting, comparing graphs, deriving inferences, drawing conclusions, developing hypotheses, etc., will enrich their graphing skills and their understanding of the functions of graphs.

For instance, students might be asked to integrate information from mixed media, such as text, tables, and graphs. Or they might be asked to compare the graph they obtained with the one they expected and make inferences about the adequacy of their data. One of the advantages of computer simulations and MBLs is that they allow more time to be spent interpreting data than is common in conventional labs. In other words, they allow students to use graphs as a starting point instead of the end point of an investigation.

Instruction should also relay the special role of graphs. The need to learn graphing skills is most apparent when instruction stresses graphs as a system for representing information in a different way from other systems. For instance, when text accompanies graphs, it should not just repeat points made by the graph: It should direct, comment, explain, and question (MacDonald-Ross, 1977). In lab activities, graphs should not always be developed from tables. There are many instances when experimental data are collected at a pace that permits students to plot their data directly onto a graph (e.g., cooling curves, titrations).

Developing students' graphing skills requires extra time and effort, but on the other hand, graphing skills can help students learn difficult science concepts. That is why we use them. It is worthwhile to spend some time along the way building graphing competence in order to enhance students' skills in learning, analyzing, and communicating. There is evidence that developing visual-spatial competence has positive effects on both understanding and motivation. The benefits will extend to other courses and to future study.

References

Balchin, W. G. V. (1972). Graphicacy. *Geography, 57,* 185–195.

Bertin, J. (1983). *Semiology of graphics: Diagrams networks maps.* (W. J. Berg, Trans.). Madison, WI: University of Wisconsin Press. (Original work published 1973).

Brasell, H. M. (1987). *Effectiveness of a microcomputer-based laboratory in learning distance and velocity graphs.* Doctoral dissertation, University of Florida, FL.

Churchill, B. E., and Goldberg, F. M. (1986). *Investigation of pre-college teachers' conceptions in kinematics.* Paper presented at the meeting of American Association of Physics Teachers, Columbus, OH.

Cleveland, W. S. (1985). *The elements of graphing data.* Monterey, CA: Wadsworth.

Goldberg, F. M., and Anderson, J. H. (in press). *Students' difficulties with negative values of kinematic quantities in graphical representations.*

Kosslyn, S. M. (1985). Graphics and human information processing. *Journal of American Statistical Association, 80,* 499–512.

Linn, M. C., Layman, J., and Nachmias, R. (1987). Cognitive consequences of microcomputer-based laboratories: Graphing skills development. *Journal of Contemporary Educational Psychology, 12,* 244–253.

MacDonald-Ross, M. (1977). How numbers are shown: A review of research on the presentation of quantitative data in texts. *Audio-Visual Communication Review, 25,* 259–409.

McDermott, L. C., Rosenquist, M. L., and Van Zee, E. H. (1987). Student difficulties in connecting graphs and physics: Examples from kinematics. *American Journal of Physics, 55,* 503–513.

Mokros, J. R., and Tinker, R. F. (1987). The impact of microcomputer-based labs on children's ability to interpret graphs. *Journal of Research in Science Teaching, 24,* 369–383.

Nachmias, R., and Linn, M. C. (1987). Evaluations of science laboratory data: The role of computer-presented information. *Journal of Research in Science Teaching, 24,* 491–506.

Pinker, S. (1981). *A theory of graph comprehension* (Occasional Paper 15). Boston, MA: Department of Psychology, Massachusetts Institute of Technology.

Schmid, C. F. (1983). *Statistical graphics: Design principles and practices.* New York: John Wiley and Sons.

Tufte, E. R. (1983). *The visual display of quantitative information*. Cheshire, CT: Graphics Press.

Van Zee, E. H., and McDermott, L. C. (1987, July). *Investigation of student difficulties with graphical representations in physics*. Paper presented at the Cornell University Second International Seminar on Misconceptions and Educational Strategies in Science and Mathematics, Cornell University.

The Uncommon Common Sense of Science

Mary Budd Rowe
University of Florida
Gainesville, Florida

Cynthia Holland
University of Florida
Gainesville, Florida

"What is this game that scientists play? They tell me that if I give something a push it will just keep on going forever or until something pushes it back to me. Anybody can see that isn't true. If you don't keep pushing, things stop. Then they say it would be true if the world were without friction, but it isn't, and if there weren't any friction how could I push it in the first place? It seems like they just change the rules all the time."

—Complaint of an "A" student.

Our brains are always trying to make sense of the world around us. The beliefs we come to have are shaped by our experiences and our interpretations of them. We develop our own explanations so quickly and naturally that we rarely recognize that the process has taken place until some event or someone's different interpretation challenges ours. These home-grown conceptions are precious to us. We cannot easily let them go or exchange them for a different explanation. But sometimes that is just what has to happen when we first study science in a more formal way in school. As we begin our studies, at least some of the results and explanations of experiments, particularly in the physical sciences, are counterintuitive.

Ideas we form from our experience in the course of living can lead us on occasion to develop intuitions that actually prevent us from being able to comprehend the prevailing explanations held by the science community. For example, our common experience of the world leads us to the Aristotelian view that the natural state of objects is to be at rest. After all, the things we set in motion eventually stop. Galileo and Newton, however, said we ought to assume that the natural state of objects is to be in motion. When something comes to rest, you should start looking for the forces that made it stop moving. Thus Galileo and Newton's point of view is counterintuitive, since it does not appear to accord with our experience. Without some compelling reasons to exchange old for new ideas the naturally grown notions stay lodged in our brains, clogging the mental and emotional filters through which we strain our experiences. As you will see in the research described below, unclogging the filters may require heroic efforts!

Each fundamental mismatch between home-grown stories about how things work and the official version taught in the classroom needs to be identified and acknowledged by students as well as their teachers. In one sense, we have here a problem involving the merging of two cultures, and it is easy for misunderstandings to develop on both sides. Students are often puzzled and angered by what seems to them to be nonsensical reasoning. Teachers are equally puzzled when what appears to them to be a perfectly good demonstration and explanation fails to effectively convince the students.

In this chapter, we describe some common misconceptions, often referred to as alternative beliefs, or even as alternative minitheories, that teachers and researchers have identified as sources of trouble, particularly in learning the physical sciences. The research confirms and reconfirms the fact that just explaining or demonstrating the science version to students is sometimes not enough to convert them to the perspective held by those in the science culture when the idea appears to conflict with their experience.

Merging Two Cultures

The process of merging cultures is never easy under any circumstances, and when it comes to physical science, there is often little incentive on the student's part to make the effort. Rather than resolve the dilemma, many of them just keep two explanations in their heads, the one they believe and the one they learn to say and do for passing tests. When M. B. Rowe questioned some very bright college freshman who had top grades in high-school physics and chemistry about why they were not continuing in science, a typical response was offered by a young man who planned to major in mathematics:

> I got the grades alright. But I knew I didn't really know. I mean I didn't really understand it. It was too messy, never clear to me. I liked it but I never could get it explained to myself so I really understood it. Sure I had grades but absolutely no confidence in what I was doing.

His comment mirrors another finding in the research: Even "A" and "B" students in college physics courses (as well as those in high-school programs) reverted to their pre-instructional conceptions, their naive intuitions, when confronted with problems in the laboratory. Time after time, researchers report that in spite of instruction a substantial number of students will use pre-instructional misconceptions to attack a problem and make predictions. This fact should make us question what tests in their present form accomplish for teachers as well as for students. Some students may be getting the right answers for the wrong reasons. It is the reasons we need to know about.

In one sense teachers, books, TV, and museums serve the dual role of travel agents for science (i.e., they attract customers and encourage investment in a journey) and guides (i.e., they speak the language of the science culture and are practiced in the ways of knowing in both cultures). One goal of instruction is to help students acquire some of the common sense characteristics of the new culture, particularly in those aspects which differ from our everyday, garden variety common sense.

Six Things to Do

There are things we can do to help students deal with counterintuitive ideas.
• We have to believe the research which confirms and reconfirms the fact that just telling and demonstrating ideas will not be enough to cause students to exchange familiar ideas for new ones.
• We have to identify what misconceptions are at work and design activities that will confront them directly. (More on this later.)
• We have to create incentive for change. That is, the ideas we present must be understandable, fruitful in a variety of contexts, and they have to exhibit

some consistency, namely, they have to hang together in some fashion that seems sensible. The challenge is to draw students into the common sense of science—which sometimes differs from the common sense of everyday life.

• Students need much more experience and active discussion in those concepts which are mismatched than with those that are consistent with scientific "story making." In short, design of instruction needs to be based in large measure on the nature of their prior knowledge.

• Students need to be let in on the situation. They will feel better (and have less damage to their confidence) if they understand how natural it is that they will have problems comprehending some new science experiences. As they become more reflective about their own learning, they may help the transformation to take place more effectively. Conversation and argument over competing explanations appears to help the transformation once students accept the notion that their task is to evaluate competing explanations, just as scientists must often do.

• We need some innovative work on testing or assessment to more nearly reflect the state of student knowledge put into action.

What Research Says

What follows is an overview of the major findings in the research on alternative conceptions or counterintuitive events in science classes. We have compiled a fairly extensive bibliography for readers who want to pursue these ideas in greater detail. The intent here is to draw out those findings and recommendations of most immediate value for instruction and curriculum purposes. There are studies of elementary, high-school, and university students. Most of the work concerns physics ideas; a lesser amount exists for chemistry and biology.

What circumstances would excite students or make them care about relationships between force and speed; or gravity and acceleration; or heat and temperature; or electricity and circuits; or conservation of matter and energy; or mass and weight; or momentum and mass, to name just a few topics that spawn counterintuitive learning issues? Students often attribute their problems to a lack of the right kind of ability when, in fact, they may just be the owners of an inappropriate set of minitheories or pre-instructional misconceptions.

M. G. Hewson (1986) and Hewson and P. W. Hewson (1983) used floating and sinking problems to examine how South African Black ninth graders linked concepts of mass, volume, and density. She found the distinction between mass and weight was missing although it had been taught on more than one occasion. Students used the two terms interchangeably, i.e., the concepts were confounded. Since they refer to different things (e.g., mass as quantity of material and weight as force) students had trouble grasping the notion of density and the dynamics of floating and sinking.

Hewson's work implies that it is necessary to distinguish among three states in which concepts might exist and to design instruction around that knowledge: (a) misconceptions, (b) incomplete or partial conceptions, and (c) confounded conceptions. Her instruction designed around these three factors produced advantages in the treatment group as compared with the group receiving the standard sequence. The fact is, however, that the amount of exchange of old for new ideas was small. Students have to be convinced that each piece of scientific "common sense" is more useful and powerful than the existing view. This is hard to achieve since student models are based on real-world experience and science models are often a step or so removed in abstractness.

M. McCloskey, A. Caramazza, and B. Green (1980) add another factor to consider, namely, how students assemble sets of ideas into consistent causal explanations. They found that African high-school students (Basatho) had home-grown explanations which, while consistent and causal in character, were not necessarily the accepted version of things. When the students studied curvilinear motion, e.g., trajectories of balls shot out of curved tubes and pendulum bobs cut loose in flight, McCloskey et al. found that students had some pieces of correct knowledge, but they assembled it in erroneous modes or wrongly invoked it. Students confused force and instantaneous velocity so they thought the path of the bobs and balls would be a compromise between the centrifugal force vector and the velocity vector. (For example, they thought that the string on the pendulum was holding the bob in, so if the string was cut while the bob was in motion, they predicted that the bob would fly out in a direct line with the string).

McCloskey et al. warns us that if naive beliefs are not unseated, the instruction may only provide students with fancier lingo for expressing these ideas. Moreover, we need to look at the linkages among the ideas. As simple and complex naive conceptions of relationships link, they become more and more resistant to change. Thus, early intervention becomes a necessity.

The findings of Hewson and McCloskey in the African context mirrors those in the United States and the United Kingdom. The ubiquitous nature of some of the misconceptions suggests that these ideas are somehow useful in everyday life with the result that students become increasingly committed to them. The degree of differentiation among the ideas and the consistency with which they are applied becomes an indicator of how intelligible, plausible, and useful the misconceptions are in the home culture. Any new story line which is counterintuitive must be perceived as having the same properties if it is to successfully displace the home-grown version.

When students give a unique explanation for each different experiment in a series, as some did in the floating/sinking study or the centrifugal force investigation, they probably have not yet acquired a stable set of generalizations. The job for teachers at the start of each unit of instruction is to find ways to characterize the belief systems of students to see how these beliefs fit with current science story making. With that in mind, teachers must design experiences and contexts for discussion that bring these beliefs out and into contention. This advice applies at either end of the academic continuum, from elementary to college level.

I. A. Halloun and D. Hestenes (1985), for example, found American college students in physics courses had misconceptions about motion and force that resembled those found by McCloskey et al. in Africa. They too noted that students often dress up their misconceptions in scientific jargon. As part of their effort to find out just how discrepant students' knowledge and views were from a key set of Newtonian concepts, they categorized those concepts as follows:
• Kinematical concepts: position, distance, motion, time, velocity, acceleration
• Dynamical concepts: inertia, force, resistance, vacuum, gravity

Halloun and Hestenes then developed an instrument to assess basic knowledge relative to the program normally offered in the first college physics course and found that initial qualitative common-sense beliefs from the home culture about motion produced a large effect on performance in physics. Conventional instruction induced only a small change in those beliefs.

One must correct the misconceptions early in the course, Halloun and Hestenes argue, or much of the rest of the material will be incomprehensible. In all cases, the diagnostic issue is to determine whether students are confounding variables, laboring under misconceptions, using embryonic notions, or having problems identifying relationships among concepts, i.e., experiencing trouble assembling a coherent story line.

Halloun and Hestenes report that natural common-sense knowledge, i.e., know-how derived from personal experience without benefit of instruction, particularly conflicts with the dynamical concepts. They not only gave the mechanics test to get a measure of qualitative understanding, they also gave a math test to get a quantitative measure. Correlation between the two measures was low; however, both tests provided good predictive validity for successful physics performance. Thus both mechanical and quantitative factors seem to play a part in physics development. Because the test items are designed to reveal misconceptions if they are present, low scores on the mechanics test does not imply that the concepts are missing; instead it implies that alternative conceptions and counterintuitive beliefs are firmly in place and may override "book" knowledge.

Move now to the other end of the age scale, three- to nine-year olds, as they cope with size, weight, and density activities as well as heat and temperature distinctions. C. Smith, S. Carey, and M. Wiser (1985) followed the evolution of some concepts from an undifferentiated array to relatively differentiated notions as children got older. The concept of weight when applied to an object, for example, moves gradually from heavy to heavy for its size. The children will eventually have to expand their notion of quantity of material and distinguish that from weight if they are to avoid the confusion already mentioned between mass and weight. Eight- and nine-year olds can make this distinction if helped. During the development period for a set of concepts their categorizations and responses to problem situations will often be inconsistent—certainly not stabilized.

Concepts which at first are diffuse, syncretic, and holistic will become differentiated and more analytic, when students are given instruction and experiences designed to help differentiation occur. Take for example the evolution of the notion of density which in the minds of children seems to be some kind of heaviness. In the Conceptually Oriented Program in Elementary Science, COPES, second graders put two clear containers, each filled with equal quantities of crisped rice cereal, on a beam balance and saw that the two weighed the same. They then grind up the cereal in one of the containers with the result that the volume of cereal is dramatically reduced, although none of the material is lost. They put the container back on the scale after first making a prediction as to whether the two containers of cereal, now of unequal volume, will still be balanced. (They are.) Activities of this kind help students differentiate concepts, i.e., grasp some of the components.

The importance of making fundamental changes in conceptions cannot be underestimated in its impact on how we interpret the world and even on what observations we make. Take as an example the changed view of the world produced when Copernicus made the sun rather than the Earth the center of his frame of reference. It changed the meaning of observations of the universe and even impacted on the philosophy and religion of the time. It is not so much that people know more, they know better; in one sense it is not so much a matter of working harder as it is a matter of working smarter.

Smith et al. note that students may also have lexical problems such as larger versus more which they say are both treated nondimensionally. Rowe (1978) reported that lexical confusion sometimes occurred because students had not internalized a distinct operational procedure to accompany each term. For example, young students repeatedly confuse soft and smooth in describing objects. She noted that students who do not confound the concepts have a separate operation attached to each term, i.e., for soft things your fingers go "up and down" but for testing smooth your fingers move back and forth across the object. Many students make that distinction automatically, but many do not. The confusion disappears when that explicit procedure is learned. In fact, she noted, a substantial number of descriptors as well as measurements in science carry with them an implicit operation which many students never learn.

According to Smith et al., children made more errors on the weight task than the size tasks, i.e., they persisted in saying "the same" when two objects were in fact different. Moreover they often said the styrofoam balls did not weigh anything. The mode of testing makes a difference in what one learns from students' behavior, and if we are not careful, we can be seriously misled—usually in the direction of underestimating the extent and nature of the knowledge. Children who had an overall weight-density conception (i.e., heavy for its size) did perfectly on verbal density tasks, but they reverted to a pure weight pattern when confronted with a forced choice involving steel and aluminum cylinders. How one asks questions can also change the outcome. For example when they asked children if shadows were made out of some kind of stuff, the answers depended on what they thought "made out of" meant.

One research issue concerns the distinction between an undifferentiated concept and one that just plain has not yet developed or at least is in a very embryonic condition. B. Perry and P. Obenauf (1987) investigated the development of qualitative concepts of motion and speed held by elementary-school students. Einstein had once asked Piaget whether first notions of the dynamical concepts, motion and speed, included the idea of speed as a function of time or if the notions were less differentiated. Piaget found that first perceptions of motion are based on stopping or starting placements. Then the notions of "path traveled" and "duration" develop. They move next to distance traveled and stopping point relations. Still later they put together duration of time needed to traverse and distance traveled. Only in the formal stage do they exhibit the ability to mentally separate and control the variables of time and distance. (Research described in this paper as well as the one by Brasell indicates that most students simply founder on confounded conceptions and misconceptions and consequently never reach a formal operational stage that will allow them to operate properly with speed and acceleration concepts.) They may first grasp speed intuitively from notions of overtaking.

Perry and Obenauf designed a test to assess development of the Piagetian hierarchy in elementary-age students. Their test coupled with the one developed by Halloun and Hestenes for college students provides a wide spectrum diagnostic tool for someone planning instruction based on Newtonian mechanics. To help sixth graders cope with Newton's second law, P. Horwitz and B. Y. White (1986) developed a set of computer simulations called "Thinkertools" that directly confronted the prevailing Aristotelian concepts held by most students with the more modern impulse theory. They used a vector approach where the student tries to guide an object on a defined path in either the x or y direction.

The interactive computer simulation teaches the idea of impulses and their relation to an object's direction of motion, changes in velocity, and change in direction. The object keeps moving in the direction of the implied impulse until acted upon by another "pulse." Each subsequent effect is governed by the direction of application of a new impulse in relation to the one which is already in effect. The simulation is designed in such a way that the effects of momentum and inertia can be explored in a frictionless world. (Our complaining "A" student would have found this program helpful. The creators plan to introduce friction into their microworld, so he would be able to investigate some of his own questions.) One anecdote which is surely a sign of the times involved the unanticipated effect of computer games in relation to some students' use of this program. When asked for suggestions that might improve Thinkertools, two students said, "Well, the creators really ought to look at PacMan. It's much faster." (There is no inertia in the PacMan world. In Thinkertools, it is built into the simulation.)

Physics teachers have always experienced trouble in getting students to make the transition from finite (the pulse) to continuous forces. Thinkertools goes from discrete forces with short duration, such as impulses, to a good approximation of uniform motion by getting students to navigate a rocket in relation to a target. The program halves the velocity increments progressively, and simultaneously halves the interval between pulses. After three or four such transformations the impulse engine closely resembles a continuously firing rocket. M. L. Rosenquist and L. C. McDermott (1987) sought to achieve similar objectives with their college students. They performed an experiment in which the changes in speed of an object appeared increasingly uniform. Students measured the separation between marks made at the beginning and end of motion for a defined period of time. The separation between dots became more and more uniform as the time interval is made shorter and shorter. In short, the instructional strategy is to move from the observation of discrete points to an understanding of uniformity in stages. They also noted that students have trouble separating position from velocity.

In another context entirely—light and images—K. Rice and E. Feher (1987) used the movement-from-discrete-points-to-uniformity strategy to help young children develop an appropriate understanding of how the physical properties of light affect what we see. To do this, they set up a fluorescent light source in the shape of a cross, and then they let the light pass through an aperture onto a screen. (Imagine a pinhole camera where you can change the size of the hole. If the opening is big, then the image on the screen is approximately the shape of the opening. But if the opening is very small then the image on the screen is the image of the crossed light source—this surprises most people—and the image is inverted.) Then they made a bunch of pinholes revealing a bunch of inverted crosses (or whatever shape light source used). They kept adding holes until gradually the overlapping crosses blend together to give the one-big-blur effect originally seen when the hole was large. This raises issues not only of shape of image but size (e.g., "The hole makes it smaller"). At first the children think the hole acts like a funnel and squeezes light down. They do not yet have the "expert" view that each point on the object gives off light in a multitude of directions. (High-school students also founder on the standard ray diagrams used to explain how images form. There are a host of misconceptions associated with light that persist into adulthood.)

Students studying electricity also have misconceptions that are not bound by the borders of a given country as D. Psillos, P. Koumaras, and O. Valassiades (1987) found. (Also see Tiberghien, Seré, Barboux, and Chomat, 1983.) The students said that in a circuit where a battery lights a bulb, the battery has something (unspecified) which it gives to the bulb, which the bulb uses in order to light up. This producer-consumer model has been found in several countries. With this model, it is not surprising that students were puzzled when they cut the wire and nothing poured out. Moreover their explanations for the electromagnetic effect around a wire—the fact that a compass needle will deflect when current flows in the wire—were consistent with their basic concept of something moving in the wire. They thought the insulation on the wire was cracked and something was getting out into the space around it.

We see in these studies a strong internal logic which is applied in a consistent manner but is not necessarily congruent with accepted explanations. S. Joshua and J. J. Dupin (1987), who also examined misconceptions in electricity, used clinical interviews and identified the same set of four misconceptions in pre-college students that N. Fredette and J. Lockhead identified in 1980.

1. Contact—a mechanical connection between a battery terminal and one light terminal is enough to describe a circuit.

2. Single wire—one wire is all you need to bring electricity from battery to bulb.

3. Clashing currents—two currents leave the battery and supply the bulb without returning to the battery.

4. Current wearing out—they may recognize circulation but the electricity somehow wears itself out. This was the main block to the attainment of a correct framework.

They note that the evolution of a new framework is not linear in the sense that the new one swallows the old. Sometimes they coexist, and each is activated or inhibited according to the situation. Sometimes the ideas are hybridized. Joshua and Dupin say that for instruction it is important to identify the ideas which are susceptible to change versus those which survive in spite of contradictory evidence. They felt the first three listed above could be changed but the last was resistant.

Exchangeable Versus Change-Resistant Concepts

Because some concepts are so resistant to change, we may be in error to suppose that direct experience and manipulation will be enough to lure students into another kind of explanation. Their initial conceptions act as a strainer for what they observe and how they draw conclusions. Many experiences, coupled with a great deal of discussion, and centered on alternative explanations, may be worth trying.

Powerful visual analogies sometimes help. Joshua and Dupin used a mechanical analogy to portray what goes on in a circuit. Imagine a set of uniform railroad cars linked end to end on a closed (circular) track—all of the track occupied by the cars. If you now push on the cars with a constant force the car-flow rate (current intensity) will be the same at all points on the track (i.e., no losses). The workers maintain the movement by tiring their muscles (energy exhaustion of the battery). So the current stays the same but the battery wears out. This paradigm, developed in response to the pattern of misconceptions they had identified, helped the students "see" relationships. Experiments are not enough, and students need help to change their interpretive stories. Every analogy has its limitations but they can provide a scaffold from which to build a more powerful conceptual framework.

As a result of D. Maloney's (1985) study of the misconceptions college students have related to conservation of mechanical energy, he recommends that instead of designing curriculum in terms of physics only, we need to design in terms of the known misconceptions. He, too, found some ideas to be exchangeable and others to be resistant. His 24-item assessment tasks were designed to show up the patterns of misconceptions as well as correct concepts. From his testing, Maloney found that there are some widely shared misconceptions or nonstandard stories that students invoke according to the situation.

We could add Maloney's assessment instrument to those developed by Hestenes and by Perry and Obenauf to give us a start on diagnosis as a basis for planning instruction.

Chemistry

In chemistry, there are far fewer studies of the kind so prevalent in the physics area. These have focused principally on the following topics: particulate nature of matter, the behavior of gases, physical and chemical changes in matter associated with conservation of mass, and the ability to balance equations. In fact, many of the studies reflect fundamental misconceptions of physical concepts.

There is confusion between chemical changes and phase changes. The mechanisms invented to explain these changes are unsatisfactory since they rely on the students' abilities to imagine events at a sub-microscopic level and then multiply them manyfold in order to connect the world they experience with the explanations. Phase changes, especially those that relate to properties of gases, are particularly troublesome. Students become confused in a morass of partial concepts and misconceptions related to pressure, temperature, volume, and conservation of motion. (See Furio Mas, Perez, and Harris,1987.) The idea that the world is full of constantly moving charged "things," miniscule in size, that travel around in spaces which are huge in comparison to their size, and that such a situation is supposed to describe objects and their changes seems—as one student put it —"fantastical." Add the notion of force fields, and their will to "make sense" of the stories we tell them vanishes. (See Ben-Zvi, Eylon, and Silberstein, 1986.)

E. E. Clough and R. Driver (1985) worked with elementary-age students in England on pressure in fluids, on heat energy, and on biological variation. They found that one must teach the particulate nature of matter if students are to understand the concept of conservation of mass. When something is gone, it is never really gone in the particulate sense. It is just someplace else. (Also see Driver, Guesne, and Tiberghien, 1985). J. D. Bradley and M. Brand (1985) report that failure of students to have an appropriate concept of the particulate nature of matter hinders their development in chemistry. Textbooks could do more with illustrations to help students grasp the particulate nature of matter in chemistry.

The concept of conservation of matter in chemical reactions relies upon a correct understanding of mass and the rearrangement of molecules (Furio Mas et al., 1987; Gussarsky and Gorodetsky, 1988). In chemistry as in physics, there is a kind of cosmic bookkeeping or accounting at work. Students can learn algorithms for balancing equations and totally miss the implications of the conservation concept in the process, failing to see, for example, its connection to problems of toxic-waste management. (See Yarroch, 1985.) Inadequate space (including volume), scale, and motion conceptions or misconceptions may be root causes of trouble in chemistry. (See, e.g., Gabel, Samuel and Hunn, 1987.)

Volume, pressure, and density difficulties appear in chemistry as well as in the physics arena, as D. L. Gabel and L. G. Enochs (1987) show in a series of investigations. There is much that needs to be done to develop good chemical intuitions, and education to that end needs to start early. It appears that the stories we tell ourselves when we are young do not go away all by themselves. Researchers find them still present in college students. It is also clear that changing the stories is no simple task. Probably the topics that produce the most persistent misconceptions need to be revisited many times over a period of years, each time with a challenge to the resistant set.

Biology

Misconception research is just now gaining some momentum in biology. At the moment much of the work concerns troubles students have with genetics. (See, e.g., Lawson and Thompson, 1988; Browning and Lehman, 1988.) The flavor of the research is very similar to that described above in that students have some well-embedded explanatory stories that cannot be easily routed out. (See, e.g., Fisher, Lipson, Hildebrand, Schoenberg, Miguel, and Porter, 1986; Fisher and Lipson, 1986; and their work with college students. Clough and Driver, 1986, did some biology investigations with young children.)

M. Browning and J. D. Lehman believe that some of the more malleable misconceptions were probably taught rather than just learned from other kinds of direct experience. The instruction may be either too simplistic, inconsistent, not well oriented to appropriate linkages of ideas, etc. These investigators developed a computer-based program to identify the nature of the conceptual maps students carry into a genetics course. Like other investigators, they found the quantitative features of genetics most troublesome for students. But they also note, as have other researchers in this area, that the vocabulary is troublesome, and how the parts are related to the whole is also very confusing. Students often have difficulty with the gamete task in meiosis, as shown in other research, suggesting that something is amiss in their understanding of meiosis. In any event, it would appear that Browning and Lehman have a diagnostic program that could provide information useful in the design of instruction in genetics.

Investigators seem to think that a great deal of conversation should be encouraged to help students identify what their stories (explanations) are and how they differ one from another and from the accepted version. Students can become co-conspirators with their teachers in achieving a transformation of concepts. Conversing freely within the scientific culture and absorption of the common-sense knowledge that marks it becomes a reasonable goal just as it is in any venture to foreign places.

References

Ben-Zvi, R., Eylon, B., and Silberstein, J. (1986). Is an atom of copper malleable? *Journal of Chemical Education, 63*(1), 64–66.

Bradley, J. D., and Brand, M. (1985). Stamping out misconceptions. *Journal of Chemical Education, 62*(4), 318.

Browning, M., and Lehman, J. D. (1988). Identification of student misconceptions in genetics problem solving via computer program. *Journal of Research in Science Teaching, 25*(9), 747–761.

Clough, E. E., and Driver, R. (1985). What do children understand about pressure in fluids? *Research in Science and Technological Education, 3*(2), 133–144.

Driver, R., Guesne, E., and Tiberghien, A. (1985). *Children's ideas in science.* Philadelphia: Milton Keynes.

Fisher, K., Lipson, J., Hildebrand, A. C., Miguel, L., Scheonberg, N., and Porter, N. (1986, February). Student misconceptions and teacher assumptions in college biology. *Journal of College Science Teaching, 15*(4) 276–280.

Fisher, K., and Lipson, J. (1986). Twenty questions about student errors. *Journal of Research in Science Teaching, 23*(9), 783–803.

Furio Mas, C. J., Perez, J. H., and Harris, H. (1987, July). Parallels between adolescents' conception of gases and the history of chemistry. *Journal of Chemical Education, 64*(7), 616–618.

Gabel, D. L., and Enochs, L. G. (1987). Different approaches for teaching volume and students' visualization ability. *Science Education, 71*(4), 591–597.

Gabel, D., Samuel, K., and Hunn, D. (1987). Understanding the particulate nature of matter. *Journal of Chemical Education, 64*(8), 695–697.

Gussarsky, E., and Gorodetsky, M. (1987). On the chemical equilibrium concept: Constrained word association and conception. *Journal of Research in Science Teaching, 25*(2), 319–333.

Fredette, N., and Lockhead, J. (1980). Student conceptions of simple circuits. *The Physics Teacher, 18*(3), 194–198.

Halloun, I. A., and Hestenes, D. (1985). Initial knowledge state of college physics students. *American Journal of Physics, 53*(11) 1043–1055.

Hewson, M. G., and Hewson, P. W. (1983). Effect of instruction using students' prior knowledge and conceptual change strategies on science learning. *Journal of Research in Science Teaching, 20*(8), 731–743.

Hewson, M. G. (1986). The acquisition of scientific knowledge: Analysis and representation of student conceptions concerning density. *Science Education, 70*(2),159–170.

Horwitz, P., and White, B. Y. (1986). *Thinkertools annual progress report.* Cambridge, MA: Bolt, Baranek, and Newman, Inc.

Joshua, S., and Dupin. J. J. (1987). Taking into account student conceptions in instructional strategy: An example in physics. *Cognition and Instruction, 4*(2), 117–135.

Lawson, A., and Thompson, L. (1988). Formal reasoning ability and misconceptions concerning genetics and natural selection. *Journal of Research in Science Teaching, 25*(9), 733–746.

Maloney, D. (1985). Rule-governed approaches to physics: Conservation of mechanical energy. *Journal of Research in Science Teaching, 22*(3), 261–278.

McCloskey, M., Caramazza, A., and Green, B. (1980). Curvilinear motion in the absence of external forces: Naive beliefs about the motion of objects. *Science, 210,* 1139–1141.

Perry, B., and Obenauf, P. (1987). The acquisition of notions of qualitative speed: The importance of spatial and temporal alignment. *Journal of Research in Science Teaching, 24*(6), 553–565.

Psillos, D., Koumaras, P., and Valassiades, O. (1987). Pupils' representations of electric current before, during and after instruction on DC circuits. *Research in Science and Technological Education, 5*(2),185–199.

Rice, K., and Feher, E., (1987). Pinholes and images: Children's conceptions of light and vision.1. *Science Education, 71*(4), 629–639.

Rosenquist, M. L., and McDermott, L. C. (1987). A conceptual approach to teaching kinematics. *American Journal of Physics, 55*(5), 407–415.

Rowe, M. B., (1978). *Teaching science as continuous inquiry* (Chapter 2). New York: McGraw–Hill.

Smith, C., Carey, S., and Wiser, M. (1985). On differentiation: A case study of the development of the concepts of size, weight, and density. *Cognition, 21,* 177–237.

Tiberghien, A., Seré, M. G., Barboux, M., and Chomat, A. (1983). *Etude des représentations presables de quelque notions de physique et leur évolution.* Rapport de rechercher, LIS RESPT, University of Paris VII.

Yarroch, W. L. (1985). Student understanding of chemical equation balancing. *Journal of Research in Science Teaching, 22*(5), 449–459.

7

The Construction and Validation of an Objective Formal Reasoning Instrument

William D. Popejoy
University of Northern Colorado
Greeley, Colorado
Gilbert M. Burney
Muscatine Community College,
Muscatine, Iowa

Science and mathematics educators increasingly use research on how students learn and reason as they plan efforts to improve student performance. This knowledge of cognitive development allows educators to help children develop their minds in a way that prepares them for later educational experiences, helps educators assess how well an activity or curriculum will be received by students, and guides educators' choices of teaching methods. In this chapter, we offer a method for determining cognitive levels which is reliable, valid, and easily administered.

Stages of Development

There are several theories of cognitive development: Chief among them, and the one we follow in this paper, postulates that children pass through a succession of identifiable stages. At each stage are marked enhancements in ability to deal with more complex learning. The Swiss psychologist Jean Piaget has been a major proponent of a stage theory of intellectual development. He divides development into four broad periods: the sensorimotor stage (0–2 years), the preoperational stage (2–7 years), the concrete operational stage (7–11 years), and the formal operational stage (11–16 years). Rates at which children pass through the stages differ. The ages listed above are only approximate ages for each stage. A stage theory of cognition has some implications for curriculum development and instruction. It implies certain questions: (a) How does the stage a student is in affect performance in science, i.e. the kinds of tasks she/he can reasonably be expected to do? (b) How can we determine whether topics and courses are placed at the correct grade level given the stages? and (c) How ought subject matter be adjusted for presentation to students at given stages of development?

A Method of Measurement

If teachers are to consider these questions, they need a method for determining cognitive levels which is valid and easily administered. The method developed by B. Inhelder and Piaget (1958) and used in many

---

investigations to measure progress toward formal thought is not practical for classroom use. Each student does a number of tasks under the supervision of a trained interviewer and, on the basis of his answers, is placed at a certain level. This method, however, presents several practical problems for teachers/researchers.

• The process is very time consuming as students must be tested individually with several tasks.

• Only certain people can do the testing, as the interviewer must be specially trained.

• Even with trained interviewers, the evaluation of an individual may vary from one interviewer to another due to the subjective nature of the evaluation. For these reasons, we have tried to construct a valid objective paper-and-pencil test to measure formal thought capabilities. In what follows, we describe what we did and present the test which we would like to have readers try.

Experience in administering the test indicates that most pupils can finish it in one class period; the fastest finish in 25–30 minutes. We would question the use of the test before grade eight; however, it has been given to bright sixth graders.

Since the test gives a global measure of how a child thinks, it can be used to guide pupils into or out of certain courses. It could be used to determine grade-placement of courses. Data based upon using the test as a pre-test would need to be gathered in each school district. For each example, if a grade of "C" or better with a success rate of 75 percent were to be accepted, it would be easy to determine a score on the test such that 75 percent of your students received a grade of "C" or better. This score could then be used for guidance purposes. Of course you might set your success rate higher or lower.

Certain units in a science course seem to be more difficult than others. This may be an indication that (a) the method of presentation does not match the cognitive level of the learners or (b) it may be that the content is so abstract (formal) that it should not be presented at all to pupils at this level. Having scores on the Burney Test available could help teachers make the necessary curriculum changes to accommodate for the cognitive level of the children in their school district.

Over 100 individuals have written for permission to use the test in formal research studies. We hope that classroom teachers can make use of it.

Background of the Instrument

Formal thought has been measured with the following types of measures
• Piagetian tasks
• tests requiring comprehension of reading passages
• logic items
• verbal and numerical analogies
• objective tests in which the items are similar to Piagetian tasks

D. Case and J. M. Collinson (1962) studied formal operations by having students read passages from texts in history, geography, and literature. The students were asked three questions for each passage. Their findings tended to support other research concerning invariant sequence of stages. In similar studies, R. N. Hallam (1967) employed test items requiring comprehension of reading passages in history, and R. Goldman (1965) used tape recorded Biblical stories. M. A. Stone (1966) used three reading passages in literature and social science. Conclusions were that comprehension and application behaviors are related to formal thought but that recall is at a lower stage.

A pencil-and-paper assessment that would classify students in the same way as the Piagetian tasks would be desirable. S. A. Hill (1960) used logic items involving sentential logic, syllogisms, and the logic of quantification. Her work was criticized by T. C. O'Brien and B. J. Shapiro (1968) who contended that her items were not content-valid. They did a follow-up study and modified the logic items to make them content-valid. W. M. Bart (1972) also has worked with logic items. His items were six-choice logic items with abstruse and absurd content. These tests had substantial content validity, modest concurrent validity, and limited construct validity.

K. R. Lovell and I. Butterworth (1966) and E. A. Lunzer (1965) used numerical and verbal analogies to measure formal reasoning. In a later study, J. W. Kincheloe (1972) constructed an instrument with 20 verbal analogies and tested fifty 11- through 18-year-old students. Kincheloe's instrument classified the students exactly as they had been classified using the pendulum task from the Piagetian protocols. In short, it represented progress in the development of another method for measuring formal thought. R. P. Tisher (1971) and W. M. Gray (1970) developed paper-and-pencil tests in which items were similar or logically equivalent to Piagetian tasks. They had moderate success with this type instrument. We set out to take advantage of the work of Kincheloe (analogies) and the Tisher and Gray verbal equivalency work.

Evaluation of the Instrument

Ninth- and 11th-grade students enrolled in the Sioux Falls, South Dakota public and Catholic schools and college freshmen enrolled at Sioux Falls College constituted the population for the study.

Test Construction. Forty-two items that were candidates for inclusion in the test to measure formal thought were constructed after a review of the literature concerning formal thought and concerning the construction of paper-and-pencil Piagetian instruments. This pool of items contained syllogisms, verbal analogies, questions involving combinatorial and probabilistic reasoning, and questions that seemed similar to Piagetian tasks in the kind of reasoning required.

These items were administered to 50 students. This sample consisted of 17 ninth graders, 17 eleventh graders, and 16 college freshmen. There were 8 male and 9 female 9th-grade subjects, 9 male and 8 female 11th-grade subjects, and 10 male and 6 female college subjects. The ages of the 9th-grade sample ranged from 14.25 to 15.5 years with the average being 14.73. The 11th-grade sample ranged in age from 16.1 to 17.2 years, with an average age of 16.6. The range of age for the college sample was 18.25 to 19.25 years with an average age of 18.9 years. A set of five Piagetian-type tasks was then administered to this same sample. The tasks were:
• the Stickman task
• the oscillation of a pendulum task
• the balance task
• the chemicals task
• three syllogisms
The biserial r correlation coefficient was computed for each paper-and-pencil item using scores on the task instrument as an outside criterion to give a value of item validity for each paper-and-pencil item. Twenty-four items were selected for the paper-and-pencil instrument to measure formal operational reasoning.

Administration of the Tests. After this final form of the objective instrument was determined it was administered to another set of students. This sample of 78 students consisted of 27 ninth graders (13 male and 14 female), 26 eleventh graders (13 male and 13 female), and 25 college freshmen (14 male and 11 female). Age ranges were 14.0 to 15.7 years for 9th graders, 16.5 to 17.3 years for 11th graders, and 18.6 to 19.5 years for college freshmen. The average age for 9th graders was 15.0 years; for 11th graders, 16.9 years; and freshmen, 19.0 years.

The Piagetian task instrument was then administered to this same sample. If the written test was performing satisfactorily it would classify students into the same category set as hands-on Piagetian tasks. The objective text was not scored until after these tasks were given to prevent bias on the part of the investigators from creeping into the situation.

Analysis of Data. Two biserial r correlation coefficients were calculated for each item on the objective instrument. One was calculated using the criterion scores (item validity) and the other was calculated using the total test scores on the objective test itself (internal consistency).

The Pearson product-moment correlation was used for a measure of concurrent validity comparing the objective instrument with the task test.

Kuder-Richardson formula #20 was used for a measure of the reliability of the objective instrument. This is the kind of statistic that helps assure you that whatever an instrument measures today it is likely to perform in the same way at another time. On the paper-pencil measure, students were classified as formal operational if they answered 17–24 items correctly, transitional if they answered 11–16 items correctly, and pre-formal if they answered 0-10 items correctly. On the five performance tasks based on Piaget and Inhelder, a student was classified as formal operational if he or she satisfactorily completed four or five tasks, transitional if he responded correctly to two or three tasks, and pre-formal if he responded correctly to zero or one task.

Results. As a result of item analysis, three of the items on the objective instrument were judged to be poor items and removed from the test appearing at the end of this chapter. The rest of the items appear valid predictors of formal thought with several having excellent predictive validity.

The Pearson product-moment correlation was used for a measure of concurrent validity comparing the objective instrument with the task instrument. Values for the 9th-grade sample, the 11th-grade sample, the college sample, and the total sample are given in Table 1.

Kuder-Richardson formula #20 was used for a measure of the reliability of the objective instrument. Reliability coefficients are reported for each grade as well as the total sample in Table 2.

Two comparisons of classification by the two instruments were made.

TABLE 1			
Concurrent Validity			
Pearson Product-Moment Correlation Coefficients			
9th grade	11th grade	13th grade	Total sample
.870	.849	.565	.853

TABLE 2			
Reliability			
Kuder-Richardson Formula # 20			
9th grade	11th grade	13th grade	Total sample
.866	.704	.528	.825

Table 3 shows that the two instruments classified students in the sample as formal or non-formal and Table 4 shows how they classified students in the sample as formal, transitional, or pre-formal.

TABLE 3			
Comparison of Classification by the Two Instruments: Method One			
88.5 % Agreement		Objective Instrument	
		Formal	Informal
Task Instrument	Formal	36	3
	Non-Formal	6	33

TABLE 4				
Comparison of Classification by the Two Instruments: Method Two				
84.6% Agreement		Objective Instrument		
		Formal	Transitional	Pre-Formal
Task Instrument	Formal	36	3	0
	Transitional	6	23	2
	Pre-Formal	0	1	7

Conclusions. Results of the study support the view that the proportion of students who can be classified as able to function at a formal operational level increases with age. Classification of 128 students by the task instrument yielded the following results: Twenty-seven percent of the 9th graders, 49 percent of the 11th graders, and 78 percent of the college freshmen were classified as formal operational.

The following conclusions were drawn from the study and are subject to the limitations of the study:
1. Adolescents who are chronologically older are more likely to exhibit formal operational thinking than those who are younger.
2. Verbal analogies of the type used in this study appear to be valid items for measurement of formal operations.

3. Certain paper-and-pencil items similar to Piagetian tasks can be used to measure formal thought with a fairly high degree of accuracy.

4. The Stickman task or other logically equivalent items have a high degree of validity for formal operations.

5. Syllogisms do not appear to be as good as other types of questions for measuring formal thought.

6. Validity and reliability coefficients indicate that there is a high correlation between the objective instrument and the task test. This means the objective test could be used in its present form to measure formal thought with a good degree of confidence that it will classify 9th and 11th graders accurately.

7. The validity and the reliability coefficients of the test when used with college freshmen are probably much better than would appear when compared with the other validity and reliability coefficients. Support for this conclusion comes from N. M. Downie (1967) who explains that one of the major determinants for the magnitude of a correlation coefficient of this type is the range of talent in the sample. He states that a moderate coefficient obtained from a fairly homogeneous group may be just as meaningful as a very high one from a group with a wide range of talent (Downie, 1967). The college group, with a large percentage at the formal operational stage, was much more homogeneous than the other groups which were spread over a wider range.

The test printed at the end of this chapter is a revision of the original test* in which three poor items, mentioned earlier, were omitted. Validity and reliability were not affected. Permission is granted in advance to photocopy and use this test for purposes of classroom testing.

---

*If anyone should wish a copy of the original 24-item test, it can be obtained by writing Dr. Gilbert Burney at Muscatine Community College, Muscatine, Iowa 52761. Please include $1.00 for the cost of mailing and processing

References

Bart, W. M. (1972). Construction and validation of formal reasoning instruments. *Psychological Reports, 30*, 663–670.

Case, D., and Collinson, J. M. (1962). The development of formal thinking in verbal comprehension. *Research Journal of Education and Psychology, 32*, 103–111.

Downie, N. M. (1967). *Fundamentals of measurement: Techniques and practices* (2nd ed.). New York: Oxford University Press.

Goldman, R. (1965). The application of Piaget's schema of operational thinking to religious story data by means of the Guttman scalogram. *British Journal of Educational Psychology, 35*, 158–169.

Gray, W. M. (1970). Children's performance on logically equivalent Piagetian tasks and written task. *Educational Research Monographs.* Dayton, OH: University of Dayton.

Hallam, R. N. (1967). Logical thinking in history. *Educational Review, 19*, 183–202.

Hill, S. A. (1960). *A study of logical abilities of children.* Unpublished doctoral dissertation, Stanford University.

Inhelder, B., and Piaget, J. (1958). *The growth of logical thinking childhood to adolescence.* New York: Basic Books.

Kincheloe, J. W. (1972). *The construction and validation of a formal thought instrument.* Unpublished doctoral dissertation, University of Northern Colorado.

Lovell, K. R., and Butterworth, I. (1966). Abilities underlying the understanding of proportionality. *Mathematics Teaching, 37,* 5–9.

Lunzer, E. A. (1965). Problems of formal reasoning in test situations. European Research in Cognitive Development *Monographs of the Society for Research in Child Development, 30,* 19–46.

O'Brien, T. C., and Shapiro, B. J. (1965). The development of logical thinking in children. *American Educational Research Journal,* 5, 531–542.

Stone, M. A. (1966). *The development of the institutional generality of formal thought.* Unpublished Doctoral dissertation, University of Illinois.

Tisher, R. P. (1971). A Piagetian questionnaire applied to pupils in a secondary school. *Child Development, 42,* 1633–1636.

LOGICAL REASONING TEST

Gilbert M. Burney

Instructions

1. For most of the questions on this test you will need only to place a cross in the space on the answer sheet like this (X). For a few of the questions, you will be asked to give two or three answers. Instructions for answering these questions will be given when they appear in the test.

2. Several questions refer to diagrams and you should examine these diagrams closely before answering these questions.

3. If you have to change an answer, erase it completely and mark the new choice.

4. Try to answer all questions; if you are not sure of an answer, then choose the one that you think is most apt to be right.

5. Think carefully before you answer each question.

1. In the diagram below, the line XYZ represents a wall and a tennis ball is hit onto the wall so that it always hits at Y. Angle 1 equals angle 6, angle 2 equals angle 5, and angle 3 equals angle 4.

If a ball bounces from Y to B it must have been hit from:
(a) A
(b) B
(c) C
(d) D
(e) E

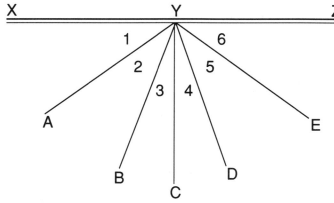

Here is a new diagram similar to the first one. Study it carefully and use it to answer questions 2 and 3.

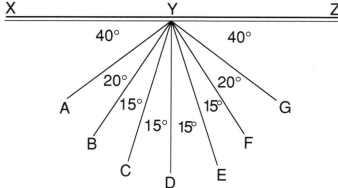

2. If a ball is hit accurately from B to Y on the wall, it will bounce to:
(a) A
(b) C
(c) E
(d) F
(e) G

3. If a ball bounces from Y to A it must have been hit from:
(a) A
(b) C
(c) E
(d) F
(e) G

4. In the diagram below, a ball is hit from A to a point Y on the wall.
The angle the new path of the ball makes with CY is:
(a) 25°
(b) 40°
(c) 50°
(d) 65°
(e) 75°

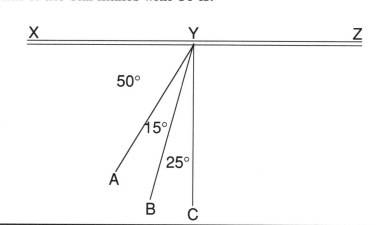

5. A tennis ball is hit from somewhere in the section marked "Right hand side" in the diagram below. The ball hits the wall at Y and bounces to C.
The size of the angle, from YZ, at which the ball must be hit is:
(a)   25°
(b)   40°
(c)   50°
(d)   60°
(e)   65°

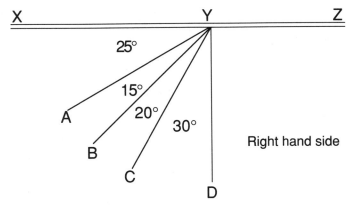

Suppose you have a balance scale similar to the one in the diagram below. Study the diagram carefully. Questions 6–7 refer to it.

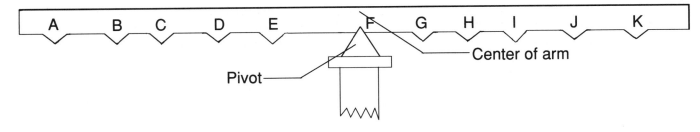

Weights which can be used:

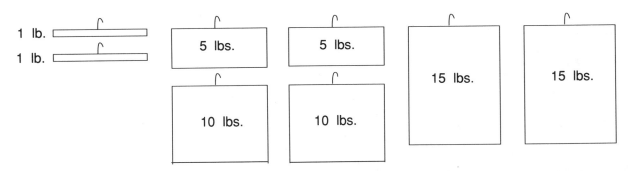

6. A five pound weight is hung at D. To balance the arm again:
(a)   a one pound weight must be hung at A.
(b)   a ten pound weight must be hung at J.
(c)   a five pound weight must be hung at H.
(d)   a ten pound weight must be hung at E.
(e)   a five pound weight must be hung at K.
(f)   is impossible.

7. A five pound weight is hung at E and a ten pound weight at C. To balance the arm again:
(a)   a five pound weight must be hung at G and a ten pound weight at J.
(b)   a ten pound weight must be hung at H and a one pound weight at K.
(c)   a fifteen pound weight must be hung at I and a one pound weight at H.
(d)   a ten pound weight must be hung at I and a five pound weight at G.
(e)   is impossible.
(f)   a five pound weight must be hung at I and a ten pound weight at G.

Questions 8–10 are called syllogisms. Each syllogism consists of two premises and a conclusion. You are to determine whether each argument is valid or not.

Example:
P[1]: No one-year-old babies can walk.
P[2]: Paul is a one-year-old baby.
_____
C: Paul cannot walk.
- - - - - - - - - - - - - - - - -
This is a valid argument.

8. P[1]: Not all R's are T's.
P[2]: All T's are M's.
_____
C: Some R's may not be M's.
(a) Valid
(b) Invalid

9. P[1]: All coal is white.
P[2]: All white coal produces red smoke when burning.
_____
C: Therefore when coal burns, the smoke is grey.
(a) Valid
(b) Invalid

10. P[1]: When Zed gets angry at Zack he hits him.
P[2]: Zed is not angry at Zack.
_____
C: Therefore Zed will not hit Zack.
(a) Valid
(b) Invalid

The diagram below represents two open-top containers with water in them. There is a length of hose connecting them that will allow water to pass from one container to the other. Container B has a larger diameter than container A. Use the diagram to answer questions 11 and 12.

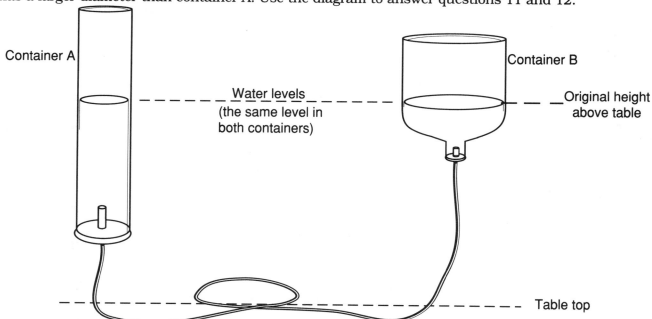

Container A

Container B

Water levels
(the same level in
both containers)

Original height
above table

Table top

11. The container A and the container B are moved down the same distance. The water levels in the containers will:
(a) stay at the original height above the table.
(b) change so that the level in A is above the original height above the table and the level in B is below.
(c) change so that the level in B is above the original height above the table and the level in A is below.
(d) change so that the levels in A and B are the same distance above the original height above the table.
(e) change so that the levels of A and B are the same distance below the original height above the table.

12. Container A and container B are moved up the same distance. The water levels in the containers will:
(a) stay at the original height above the table.
(b) change so that the levels in A and B are the same distance below the original height above the table.
(c) change so that the level in A is above the original height above the table and the level in B is below.
(d) change so that the levels in A and B are the same distance above the original height above the table.
(e) change so that the level in B is above the original height above the table and the level in A is below.

The apparatus pictured below can be used to throw shadows onto a screen. The rings pictured can be placed at points D, E, or F or anywhere along a line through D, E, and F between the light and the screen. The shadows that are referred to in the questions are the circular shadows of the rings only, not the ring stands. The distances of D, E, and F from the screen are indicated above and the distances of D, E, and F from the light are indicated below the apparatus. Study the diagram carefully and use it to answer questions 13–14.

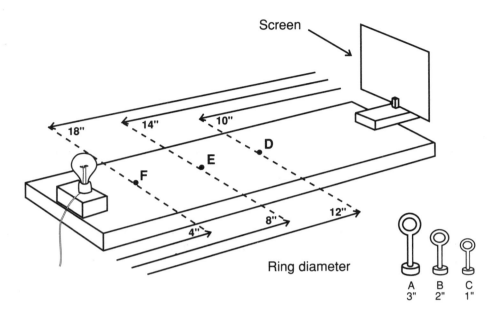

13. The ring A is placed at D and its shadow allowed to fall onto the screen and the size of the shadow is measured. Ring A is removed and ring B is placed at D and the size of its shadow on the screen is measured. The two shadows formed:
(a) will be of equal size.
(b) will be of unequal size, the shadow of A being larger than the shadow of B.
(c) will be of unequal size, the shadow of B being larger than the shadow of A.
(d) will be of unequal size, the shadow of A being smaller than the shadow of B.

14. The ring B is placed at D and its shadow allowed to fall onto the screen and the size of the shadow is measured. Ring B is removed and ring C is placed at D and the size of its shadow on the screen is measured. The two shadows formed:
(a) will be of equal size.
(b) will be of unequal size, the shadow of B being larger than the shadow of C.
(c) will be of unequal size, the shadow of C being larger than the shadow of B.
(d) will be of unequal size, the shadow of B being smaller than the shadow of C.

The diagram below represents two glasses, a small one and a large one, and two jars, a small one and a large one. Use this diagram for problem 15.

15. If it takes six large glasses of water or nine small glasses of water to fill the small jar and it takes eight large glasses of water to fill the large jar, then how many small glasses of water does it take to fill the large jar?
(a) 10
(b) 11
(c) 12
(d) 15
(e) 16

Questions 16–21 are verbal analogies. Verbal analogies consist of two pairs of words with each pair having the same relationship. In is to out as up it to down is an example of an analogy. The common relationship between in-out and up-down is that they are opposites. Order of the pair of words is also important. Peel is to banana as paint is to house is correct while peel is to banana as house is to paint is incorrect. In the following questions you are to choose two or three words that will best complete each analogy.

Example:

(a)	tire	is to	car	as	(e)	anchor	is to	ship
(b)	motor				(f)	deck		
(c)	highway				(g)	captain		
(d)	motor				(h)	ocean		

In this example, the best choice to complete the analogy are highway and ocean resulting in the analogy highway is to car as ocean is to ship. In this case "operates on" is the common relationship, a car operates on a highway and a ship operates on the ocean. On the answer sheet the above question would be answered as shown below.

a	b	c	d		e	f	g	h
( )	( )	(X)	( )		( )	( )	( )	(X)

Be careful to mark all required answers for each question on the answer sheet.
Some questions require two answers and some require three.

16.

	Task	is to	(a)	attempt	as	(e)	problem	is to	solution
			(b)	completion		(f)	chemical		
			(c)	work		(g)	man		
			(d)	question		(h)	answer		

17.

	Light bulb	is to	(a)	switch	as	(e)	engine	is to	(i)	boat
			(b)	wire		(f)	canoe		(j)	engine
			(c)	socket		(g)	motor		(k)	tractor
			(d)	electricity		(h)	steam		(l)	paddle

18.

(a)	walk	is to	body	as	wheel	is to	(e)	roll
(b)	toe						(f)	machine
(c)	knee						(g)	bicycle
(d)	foot						(h)	spokes

19.

(a)	cow	is to	flock	as	(e)	soldier	is to	(i)	bee
(b)	horse				(f)	swarm		(j)	pig
(c)	sheep				(g)	pack		(k)	regiment
(d)	foot				(h)	litter		(l)	wolf

NATIONAL SCIENCE TEACHERS ASSOCIATION

20.

(a)	brain	is to	head	as	(e)	spring	is to	(i)	bedpost
(b)	eye				(f)	blanket		(j)	ticking
(c)	hat				(g)	caster		(k)	bed
(d)	ear				(h)	pillow		(l)	summer

21.

(a)	music	is to	piano	as	(e)	chair	is to	table
(b)	house				(f)	leg		
(c)	bench				(g)	eat		
(d)	tuner				(h)	furniture		

Logical Reasoning Answer Sheet

1. a   b   c   d   e
   ( )   ( )   ( )   ( )   ( )

2. a   b   c   d   e
   ( )   ( )   ( )   ( )   ( )

3. a   b   c   d   e
   ( )   ( )   ( )   ( )   ( )

4. a   b   c   d   e
   ( )   ( )   ( )   ( )   ( )

5. a   b   c   d   e
   ( )   ( )   ( )   ( )   ( )

6. a   b   c   d   e   f
   ( )   ( )   ( )   ( )   ( )   ( )

7. a   b   c   d   e   f
   ( )   ( )   ( )   ( )   ( )   ( )

8. a   b
   ( )   ( )

9. a   b
   ( )   ( )

10. a   b
   ( )   ( )

11. a   b   c   d   e
   ( )   ( )   ( )   ( )   ( )

12. a   b   c   d   e
   ( )   ( )   ( )   ( )   ( )

13. a   b   c   d
   ( )   ( )   ( )   ( )

14. a   b   c   d
   ( )   ( )   ( )   ( )

15. a   b   c   d   e
   ( )   ( )   ( )   ( )   ( )

16. a   b   c   d   e   f   g   h
   ( )   ( )   ( )   ( )   ( )   ( )   ( )   ( )

17. a   b   c   d   e   f   g   h   i   j   k   l
   ( )   ( )   ( )   ( )   ( )   ( )   ( )   ( )   ( )   ( )   ( )   ( )

18. a   b   c   d   e   f   g   h
   ( )   ( )   ( )   ( )   ( )   ( )   ( )   ( )

19. a   b   c   d   e   f   g   h   i   j   k   l
   ( )   ( )   ( )   ( )   ( )   ( )   ( )   ( )   ( )   ( )   ( )   ( )

20. a   b   c   d   e   f   g   h   i   j   k   l
   ( )   ( )   ( )   ( )   ( )   ( )   ( )   ( )   ( )   ( )   ( )   ( )

21. a   b   c   d   e   f   g   h
   ( )   ( )   ( )   ( )   ( )   ( )   ( )   ( )

NATIONAL SCIENCE TEACHERS ASSOCIATION

Logical Reasoning Answer Key

See Errata at the front of this book.

1. a ( ) b ( ) c ( ) d (X) e ( )

2. a ( ) b ( ) c ( ) d (X) e ( )

3. a ( ) b ( ) c ( ) d ( ) e (X)

4. a ( ) b (X) c ( ) d ( ) e ( )

5. a ( ) b ( ) c ( ) d (X) e ( )

6. a ( ) b ( ) c (X) d ( ) e ( ) f ( )

7. a ( ) b ( ) c ( ) d (X) e ( ) f ( )

8. a (X) b ( )

9. a ( ) b (X)

10. a ( ) b (X)

11. a ( ) b ( ) c ( ) d ( ) e (X)

12. a ( ) b ( ) c ( ) d (X) e ( )

13. a ( ) b (X) c ( ) d ( )

14. a ( ) b (X) c ( ) d ( )

15. a ( ) b ( ) c (X) d ( ) e ( )

16. a ( ) b (X) c ( ) d ( ) e (X) f ( ) g ( ) h ( )

17. a ( ) b ( ) c ( ) d (X) e ( ) f (X) g ( ) h ( ) i ( ) j ( ) k ( ) l (X)

18. a ( ) b ( ) c ( ) d (X) e ( ) f ( ) g (X) h ( )

19. a ( ) b ( ) c (X) d ( ) e (X) f ( ) g ( ) h ( ) i ( ) j ( ) k (X) l ( )

20. a ( ) b ( ) c (X) d ( ) e ( ) f (X) g ( ) h ( ) i ( ) j ( ) k (X) l ( )

21. a ( ) b ( ) c (X) d ( ) e (X) f ( ) g ( ) h ( )

What Research Says to the Science Teacher: The Process of Knowing

Correction for page 115

You will need the following material to score Gilbert M. Burney's Logical Reasoning Test.

In order to be counted correct, questions 6–12 must be marked exactly as they appear on the answer key.

Rate the students' scores by the number of correct answers.

Formal: 15–21
Transitional: 10–14
Pre-Formal: 0–9